Practical Guide to SAP® HANA and Big Data Analytics

Dominique Alfermann
Stefan Hartmann

Thank you for purchasing this book from Espresso Tutorials!

Like a cup of espresso coffee, Espresso Tutorials SAP books are concise and effective. We know that your time is valuable and we deliver information in a succinct and straightforward manner. It only takes our readers a short amount of time to consume SAP concepts. Our books are well recognized in the industry for leveraging tutorial-style instruction and videos to show you step by step how to successfully work with SAP.

Check out our YouTube channel to watch our videos at
https://www.youtube.com/user/EspressoTutorials.

If you are interested in SAP Finance and Controlling, join us at
http://www.fico-forum.com/forum2/
to get your SAP questions answered and contribute to discussions.

Related titles from Espresso Tutorials:

- ▶ Rob Frye, Joe Darlak, Dr. Bjarne Berg: The SAP® BW to HANA Migration Handbook
  http://5109.espresso-tutorials.com
- ▶ Dominique Alfermann, Stefan Hartmann, Benedikt Engel: SAP® HANA Advanced Modeling
  http://5110.espresso-tutorials.com
- ▶ Christian Savelli: SAP® BW on SAP HANA
  http://5128.espresso-tutorials.com
- ▶ Deepa Rawat: Practical Guide to Advanced DSOs in SAP®
  http://5213.espresso-tutorials.com
- ▶ Frank Riesner, Klaus-Peter Sauer: SAP® BW/4HANA and BW on HANA
  http://5215.espresso-tutorials.com
- ▶ Bert Vanstechelman: The SAP® HANA Implementation Guide
  http://5289.espresso-tutorials.com

Dominique Alfermann, Stefan Hartmann
Practical Guide to SAP® HANA and Big Data Analytics

ISBN:	978-3-96012-621-8
Editor:	Karen Schoch
Cover Design:	Philip Esch
Cover Photo:	belov1409, #103708329 — stock.adobe.com
Interior Book Design:	Johann-Christian Hanke

All rights reserved.

1st Edition 2018, Gleichen

© 2018 by Espresso Tutorials GmbH

URL: *www.espresso-tutorials.com*

All rights reserved. Neither this publication nor any part of it may be copied or reproduced in any form or by any means or translated into another language without the prior consent of Espresso Tutorials GmbH, Bahnhofstr. 2, 37130 Gleichen, Germany.

Espresso Tutorials makes no warranties or representations with respect to the content hereof and specifically disclaims any implied warranties of merchantability or fitness for any particular purpose. Espresso Tutorials assumes no responsibility for any errors that may appear in this publication.

Feedback
We greatly appreciate any kind of feedback you have concerning this book. Please mail us at *info@espresso-tutorials.com*.

Table of Contents

Foreword   7
    Personal dedication   8

1 Introduction   11
    1.1 Intention   11
    1.2 Objective   12
    1.3 Target audience   13
    1.4 In scope/out of scope   13
    1.5 Content   14
    1.6 Definition of terms   15

2 Building blocks of an SAP HANA architecture   17
    2.1 SAP HANA functionalities   20
    2.2 SAP S/4HANA Embedded Analytics   33
    2.3 SAP BW/4HANA   38
    2.4 Data provisioning tools   46
    2.5 Analytics components   53
    2.6 Front-end tools   60
    2.7 Big Data ecosystems   69
    2.8 Cloud platforms   77
    2.9 Summary   83

3 SAP HANA BI architectures   85
    3.1 SAP HANA BI reference architecture   85
    3.2 SAP HANA native   88
    3.3 SAP BW/4HANA   102
    3.4 SAP HANA merged with Big Data   114
    3.5 SAP HANA merged with analytics   128
    3.6 SAP HANA in the cloud   141

	3.7	SAP HANA mixed scenarios	148
	3.8	Migration scenarios	169
	3.9	Architecture decision matrix and best practices	176
	3.10	Summary	180
4	**Organizational principles**		**183**
	4.1	Landscape enablement	183
	4.2	Data Governance	187
	4.3	Development environment	193
	4.4	Data security and authorizations	200
	4.5	Change process and training	208
	4.6	Summary	214
5	**Summary and outlook**		**217**
	5.1	Summary	217
	5.2	Outlook	221
A	**About the Authors**		**228**
B	**Index**		**229**
C	**Disclaimer**		**233**

Foreword

In today's world, technologies are evolving at an extraordinary pace and new market opportunities are developing just as quickly. Companies face the challenge of adapting to unfamiliar technologies and markets with different rules and key players. While businesses adapt, IT departments face similar struggles with constantly changing business requirements and new technologies. In these hectic times, it is essential to have a good business intelligence foundation in order to keep track of both new and existing business.

SAP is one of the big players in business software and is currently developing new products and promoting new product suites at a speed previously unknown to most customers. Additionally, traditional SAP-based companies now need to combine their SAP systems with non-SAP-based software more than ever before, e.g. in the context of Big Data. New possibilities to maintain and provide company software, such as cloud platforms make architecture decisions more complicated, but also enable new business scenarios. The complexity lies in understanding the different architecture possibilities and deciding on the best option for your company.

This book aims to deliver clear recommendations for building a solid architecture based on the latest SAP HANA technologies; with an additional focus on the combination with Big Data platforms. We provide a detailed assessment of several possible architecture scenarios, a guideline on how to decide on one option or another, principles for processes, and the organization around such an architecture.

The target audience of this book is mainly SAP BI and Big Data architects, as well as IT architects. However, we welcome anyone else to dive with us into the wide world of SAP HANA BI opportunities. Readers should have a fundamental understanding of how a data warehouse functions, and the associated technologies, as well as a familiarity with Big Data environments.

Personal dedication

This book is the result of a great deal of encouragement, support and contribution from friends, families, and colleagues. Their numerous ideas, hints, and discussions helped us to greatly enrich each chapter. We would specifically like to mention Bikas Panigrahi who provided valuable input during the course of writing this book.

Last but not least, we want to say thank you to the Espresso Tutorials team, especially to Alice Adams, who patiently advised us in formalizing and completing the book.

We have added a few icons to highlight important information. These include:

Tips

Tips highlight information that provides more details about the subject being described and/or additional background information.

Examples

Examples help illustrate a topic better by relating it to real world scenarios.

Attention

Attention notices highlight information that you should be aware of when you go through the examples in this book on your own.

Finally, a note concerning the copyright: all screenshots printed in this book are the copyright of SAP SE. All rights are reserved by SAP SE. Copyright pertains to all SAP images in this publication. For the sake of simplicity, we do not mention this specifically underneath every screenshot.

1 Introduction

In this chapter, we highlight the reasons for writing this book and we explain the scope and content. We conclude the chapter by defining frequently used terms.

1.1 Intention

A key element for successful company management is a solid Business Intelligence (BI) solution, including a constant, up-to-date and holistic view of all business processes. A comprehensive BI platform provides decision makers at all levels of management with crucial reports and analyses for evaluating the current state of their organization, specifically the area they are responsible for. The underlying data basis has changed significantly in recent years. At the beginning, intra-company data was loaded via batch processing on a nightly basis. Now, BI (according to the definition in this book) includes external data, the processing of data in real-time, on-the-fly calculation of statistical models, and quick, user-friendly, well-defined reports; all with only a few clicks.

This evolution stems mostly from technical capabilities created by large-scale, in-memory computing, volume and velocity provided by distributed computing clusters, scalability, and advancements in UI out-of-the-box solutions. These technological developments have led to completely new business models, such as social media platforms, and cloud providers, and also to new technical solutions such as Big Data platforms, sensor analytics and real-time reporting. With these technical developments, you have the possibility for a much more elaborate business process analysis, also taking external information into account.

Suddenly, companies have the ability to tap into large social networks, delivering product opinions and trends on a scale never seen before. Weather data can be constantly evaluated in order to calculate better transport routes in logistics, or take storms and earthquakes into account for business and risk calculations.

However, in order to fully benefit from these new BI opportunities, you need a solid technical foundation together with a pervasive organizational change management within the company. Several questions need to be answered and decisions have to be made:

- ▶ Which technologies are best used within my company in order to reap all the described benefits?
- ▶ How do these technologies integrate in a consistent manner?
- ▶ What architectural principles should be followed during implementation, especially with a combination of technologies?
- ▶ How do I have to adapt my organization to fully leverage the capabilities of these new technologies?

These are just some examples of the fundamental questions that you need to address. Today, many vendors supply tools for comprehensive BI reporting and analysis, as well as for Big Data and in-memory computing. One of the vendors providing a consistent, integrated BI solution is SAP. Their portfolio, originally only simple SAP BW technology, has been significantly expanded over recent years. You now find new and improved products for reporting (e.g. SAP Lumira, Analysis for Office, SAP Design Studios etc.), for in-memory computing (e.g. SAP HANA), for predictive analytics (e.g. SAP Predictive Analytics suite), and for data warehousing and Extraction, Transformation and Load (ETL) operations (e.g. SAP BW, SAP Data Services etc.). In addition, connectors to Big Data environments have been continuously enhanced.

In this book, we provide a clear view of the latest technology trends in the SAP-based BI area, especially in conjunction with non-SAP Big Data technologies. Building on our project and lab experience, we give answers and recommendations on how various technological components can be combined in the most efficient and architecturally sound way in order to fulfill your company's analytics needs.

1.2 Objective

Our goal in this book is to provide clear recommendations for building a solid architecture based on the latest SAP HANA technologies; combination with Big Data platforms included. We provide a detailed assessment of several possible architecture scenarios, a guideline on how to decide on one or the other, principles for processes, and the organization around such architecture.

1.3 Target audience

This book is aimed at SAP BI and Big Data architects, as well as IT personnel responsible for future-proof analytics solutions; but anyone is welcome to dive with us into the wide world of SAP HANA BI opportunities. Readers should have a fundamental understanding of how a data warehouse functions, and its associated technologies, as well as the technologies related to Big Data environments.

1.4 In scope/out of scope

This publication aims to establish a solid decision basis for your company's SAP HANA-based BI architecture by providing recommendations and best practices following the latest SAP product and technology trends. These recommendations include:

1. general architecture scenarios consisting of an SAP HANA native data warehouse, an SAP BW/4HANA data warehouse (including SAP S/4HANA Embedded Analytics), a Big Data platform with a focus on SAP integrative use cases, an Advanced Analytics solution, and mixed scenarios;
2. individual architecture scenarios with a mix of the above-mentioned solution components;
3. a decision matrix to assist in selecting the best architecture components and how to reach this decision, and
4. structuring your organization and its processes in order to facilitate the breadth and complexity of your technical architecture with the different components.

The recommendations for the defined scope result from project experience, lab sessions, and the authors' extensive work with these technologies.

This book does not cover non-SAP-based data warehouse solutions (excluding Big Data-based solutions), or detailed front-end integration evaluation. We focus purely on the latest SAP technologies and specifically exclude outdated SAP BW objects (such as InfoCube), SAP HANA 1.0 attribute and analytical views, and SAP ERP/Suite on HANA with SAP HANA Live.

1.5 Content

This book is organized in a logical sequence to help you explore the various architecture options, associated technologies and organizational principles related to SAP HANA BI architectures. We begin with an overview of relevant architectural elements and technologies in SAP HANA BI and Big Data platforms (in conjunction with SAP HANA). Next, we build on these elements by combining them with possible architectural scenarios and options. This includes a decision matrix of how to find the right scenario for your individual needs. Finally, based on the new technologies and architectures relevant for your individual needs, we look at the impact on your organization itself, and the related processes. We close with an overall summary and an overview of further topics resulting from the points covered in this book.

Let us have a brief look at the chapter content.

Chapter 2 looks at the latest technologies used within an SAP-based BI Architecture. As the core element of any current SAP data warehouse architecture is SAP HANA, we named the chapter accordingly. It contains core SAP HANA features and introduces the reader to the latest Big Data technologies and to the current SAP HANA-based integration possibilities with Big Data environments. We continue by explaining possible cloud scenarios and service models before we switch over to the possible front-end tools that operate with SAP and Big Data platforms. The last part of this chapter looks at the various solutions available for ETL in its different forms for Big Data platforms, as well as for data warehouses.

Chapter 3 combines the components presented in Chapter 2 and merges them into solid architectural scenarios. Determining which scenario best fits your individual needs depends on your previously identified requirements. The first section of this chapter discusses details of an SAP

BW/4HANA-based architecture scenario. We continue with an SAP HANA native scenario, describing the advantages and challenges when implementing an SAP HANA native data warehouse. These two sections lead to a detailed discussion on how SAP HANA can most efficiently be merged with a Big Data platform. In addition, we focus on predictive analytics platforms utilizing the SAP HANA database and cloud implementations for all scenarios. We finish with best practices for a migration and a decision matrix, as well as best practices for deciding on the right architecture scenario.

Chapter 4 continues with organizational and procedural changes resulting from the move to a new BI architecture. We introduce the topic of landscape enablement, which includes subjects such as sizing, BI roadmap visioning, interfaces, and components. The next section moves into the area of governance, especially Data Governance with its required roles, responsibilities, and processes. Next, we discuss parallel development in a highly integrated environment, end-to-end testing, and debugging. We conclude with recommendations for security, authorization, and change processes, including training approaches for your existing team.

Chapter 5 provides a summary of the previous chapters and takes a look at further topics that should be investigated. We also outline what we see next on the horizon for SAP HANA BI eco systems. This chapter specifically refers to the latest SAP developments; e.g. SAP Leonardo and SAP Data Hub.

1.6   Definition of terms

Most of our technological terms are explained in Chapter 2, but there are additional, fundamental terms that we outline here.

Let us start with **Business Intelligence (BI)**. Within the context of this book, BI is defined as all methods for gathering, analyzing, evaluating and reporting data. Furthermore, we view Big Data platforms, used for data analysis, as part of Business Intelligence. For the purposes of this book, the term Business Intelligence includes all technologies related to data gathering, analysis and evaluation.

As part of BI, **data warehouses** are data storage platforms, optimized for the analysis of structured data which has been gathered from several sources. They usually combine data in order to fulfill individual reporting needs.

The term **Extraction, Transformation and Loading (ETL)** describes processes used for gathering data from several sources and writing them into a platform optimized for reporting. As the term implies, data is extracted from a source system, transformed and enriched with additional information, and then loaded into the target system. In recent years, especially with in-memory and Big Data platforms becoming more popular, the term has been slightly changed to ELT (Extract, Load, Transform). This involves the same processes, but in a different order, resulting in a better use of power in in-memory and Big Data environments for the execution of transformations with massive amounts of data.

Finally, the most important explanations in this book are for the terms **BI architecture** and **architecture scenarios**. We define architecture as an overall framework, which provides standards and policies to structure BI tools and associated developments, thereby helping to define the mainstays of your future BI ecosystem. We specifically exclude infrastructure requirements from this term, as it is not the focus of this book. We define architectural options for SAP HANA BI-related scenarios as individual options for fulfilling your specific reporting needs. In doing so, we introduce solid architectures while combining selected tools and technologies. In the best case, a described scenario can cover all your reporting or analysis requirements without requiring further tools and technologies.

2 Building blocks of an SAP HANA architecture

This chapter introduces you to the specific building blocks of the architecture scenarios that we explore and use for our architectural discussions throughout this book. We present you with SAP-specific technology and tools, as well as non-SAP tools that we believe fit well into a modern overall BI architecture. Each section provides an explanation of the tools, recommendations for their usage and further information.

Table 2.1 provides an overview of the tools we discuss in this chapter, and gives links to information on technologies that are relevant for architectural (SAP HANA) designs.

Component	Description	Reference
SAP HANA core features		
SAP HANA server-side components	The components of an SAP HANA server such as index, name, statistic server, etc.	See *SAP HANA Advanced Modeling*
SAP HANA engines	Similar functionalities are bundled into engines	See Section 2.1.2
SAP HANA rules framework	Business rules can be defined by the end user	https://blogs.sap.com/2016/12/19/hana-rules-framework-hrf-blog-of-blogs
Extended applications services advanced (XSA)	The XSA engine sustains several SAP HANA internal applications and also builds the basis for web apps	See Section 2.1.3
SAP HANA deployment infrastructure	HDI uses containers to package functionality into one single application	See Section 2.1.4

Component	Description	Reference
SAP HANA Views	SAP HANA views are used to combine data for reporting	See Section 2.1.5
Libraries (PAL, BFL, AFL, etc.)	Libraries represent standard functionality that can be reused within SAP HANA	See Section 2.1.6
Building your SAP HANA BI architecture		
Big Data technologies	Tools for managing and running a Big Data platform	See Section 2.7
Predictive analytics tools	Tools used for finding patterns in, and making predictions on, the data	See Section 2.4
SAP BO/HANA in the cloud	Using cloud computing for running SAP HANA and SAP BusinessObjects	See Section 2.8
Front-end tools	Tools for the visualization and reporting of data (e.g. SAP Lumira)	See Section 2.6
Data provisioning tools	Tools for the provisioning of data (e.g. SAP Data Services, Kafka, etc.)	See Section 2.4
SAP BW/4HANA	SAP data warehousing component running only on SAP HANA	See Section 2.3
Around SAP HANA BI architectures		
SAP S/4HANA	New operational system for different Lines of Business optimized for SAP HANA	See Section 2.2
SAPS/4HANA Embedded Analytics	Operational reporting component for S/4HANA modules only	See Section 2.2
SAP HANA dynamic tiering	Support of the data temperature concept including storage via Big Data	*https://blogs.sap.com/ 2018/04/18/whats-new-sap-hana-dynamic-tiering-2.0-sp-03*

Component	Description	Reference
SAP Edge Services	Internet of Things (IoT) data collection at the point of creation instead of at a central SAP HANA server	https://www.sap.com/products/edge-services.html
SAP HANA Data Warehousing Foundation	Manage data and memory efficiently across the application landscape	https://blogs.sap.com/2015/03/04/sap-hana-data-warehousing-foundation/
SAP HANA real-time replication	Real-time replication based on the SAP Landscape Transformation Replication Server (SLT)	https://blogs.sap.com/2017/02/01/sap-hana-2.0-editions-and-options-by-the-sap-hana-academy/
SAP Business Suite on HANA	SAP modules running on SAP HANA, not yet on S/4HANA	https://blogs.saphana.com/2014/08/29/the-benefits-of-the-business-suite-on-hana/
Change and Transport System (CTS+) and SAP HANA Transport for ABAP (HTA)	Transport of SAP HANA and ABAP managed objects	A useful guide for these tools can be found here: https://blogs.sap.com/2015/06/11/cts-or-hta/
Intelligent Enterprise	SAP HANA Analytics plays an essential role, achieving an effective use of data throughout the enterprise	https://www.sap.com/products/intelligent-enterprise.html

Table 2.1: Overview of SAP HANA related tools

Before looking into each component, we will first introduce a high-level view of our reference architecture that is further detailed in Chapter 3.

Following this layer architecture, we will look at the essential building blocks of an SAP-centric BI landscape in today's world (Figure 2.1).

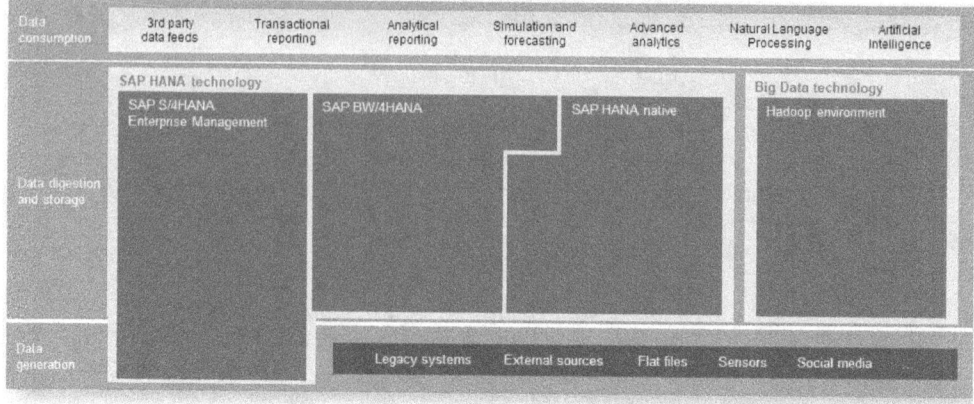

Figure 2.1: Reference layers of a BI landscape

Data generation is the sourcing layer of all data we plan to process in our BI landscape. Looking at the SAP world, SAP S/4HANA is a good example of this. In the *data digestion and storage layer*, data is processed, pre-calculated and stored for further use. SAP BW/4HANA, SAP HANA native or Big Data technologies provide significant features to implement this layer. Last, but not least, *data consumption* gives access to the data processed in the previous layers.

2.1 SAP HANA functionalities

This section introduces the SAP HANA related add-ons and features that are the most relevant for designing an SAP HANA-based BI architecture. This specifically excludes data provisioning tools, analytical tools and frontends, which are discussed separately in the following sections.

2.1.1 SAP HANA 2.0

In December 2016, SAP released SAP HANA 2.0—the digital foundation to build the next-generation of analytics applications. In the following section, we highlight selected innovations and new features of this version.

First, let's start with the migration path. With SAP HANA 1.0 SPS 10 or higher, an upgrade to SAP HANA 2.0 SPS 00 can be performed directly. When migrating from SPS 12, you can test SAP HANA 2.0 SPS 00 with the capture and replay function before migrating. If you run SAP HANA 1.0 SPS 9 or older, you need to upgrade to SAP HANA 1.0 SPS 12 first.

One of the new features in SAP HANA 2.0 is the *Active/Active (read-enabled)* option, where a secondary SAP HANA system (which is synchronized with the primary through logs) is utilized to take over read-intensive processes. Whereas read and write operations are executed only on the primary SAP HANA system, the second one acts autonomously in answering queries (read operations).

Active/Active (read-enabled) option—SAP S/4HANA case

A good example of an SAP S/4HANA system (see Section 2.2.1) which uses the Active / Active read-enabled option can be found at:

https://blogs.sap.com/2017/06/22/making-use-of-an-activeactive-read-only-hana-database-in-s4-hana/

Furthermore, and especially against the background of General Data Protection Regulation (GDPR) in Europe, *data security and authorization management* (e.g. on LDAP groups) has improved. New encryption features have been released (e.g. full native data at rest encryption, enhanced encryption key management).

Workload management helps SAP HANA 2.0 to better avoid system-overload situations. Requests can be automatically rejected from the database when a threshold is exceeded.

With regard to *data integration* features, the Smart data integration (SDI), Smart data quality, and Smart data access components have been enhanced. For instance, SDI now allows virtual procedures (e.g. via BAPI) to perform read/write operations with ABAP-based systems.

In the *streaming area*, messages are now guaranteed via REST interface. In a real-time analysis scenario, data delivery is now ensured. New adaptors like oDATA and JSON enable greater flexibility.

Regarding administration, *SAP HANA Cockpit* has been re-architected and now also supports on-premise and cloud implementations. Database management has been unified.

There are many other changes and features available with SAP HANA SPS 00; for example, new solutions, improvements, and component reforms relating to Workload Capture and Replay, Backup and Recovery, SAP Enterprise Architecture Designer (Edition for SAP HANA), Dynamic Tiering, Predictive Analytics Library, High Availability and the SAP HANA Extended Application Services (see also Section 2.1.3).

SAP HANA 2.0 features

The following blog offers a good starting point to identify the major changes, which come with SAP HANA 2.0 SPS 00: *https://blogs.sap.com/2016/12/01/whats-new-with-sap-hana-2.0-sps-00-by-the-sap-hana-academy/*.

New support packages and stacks (SPS) for SAP HANA 2.0 are released twice a year, and the latest information and updates are available at:
https://www.sap.com/products/hana/features/whats-new.html.

2.1.2 SAP HANA engines

The engines within SAP HANA build the foundation for any application running on the SAP HANA platform. The development of the SAP HANA engines started with the first SAP HANA revision and continuously evolved during further revisions. SAP HANA started out with the following engines: join, calculation, SQL, Online Analytical Processing (OLAP), row, column and XS. The importance of these engines, as well as the engines themselves, has gradually changed. From a definition perspective, it is hard to say what exactly constitutes an engine. When reading different lists of the SAP HANA platform features, further engines are mentioned. These include the spatial, the graph, and the planning engines; and depending on the definition of "engine", we could even say there is a "predictive" engine. We will take a closer look at the SQL engine in the following section. Further detail about the predictive and spatial options can be found in Section 2.4.

The SAP HANA engines

 For detailed information on the SAP HANA engines, we recommend reading our book *SAP HANA Advanced Modeling*.

Important functionalities of SAP HANA are the modeling of views, the execution of SQL statements within the database for checking results, and the ability to write more complex programming logic. In these cases, the *SQL engine* is utilized.

First, we need to take a step back and have a quick look at SAP HANA views. SAP started out by distinguishing attribute, analytical and calculation views in the first Service Packs. In the last two years, we have noticed a clear movement towards using only calculation and scripted SQL views. In addition, SAP has not only been promoting the use of Core Data Services (CDS) views to the customer, but has also been promising to build future extractors and embedded analytics for S/4HANA based on CDS views.

CDS views, like calculation views, are based on SQL. Due to this development, we believe that the SQL engine should be explained in more detail here.

So how does the SQL engine work? The SQL engine does not simply take SQL code and query the referenced objects within it. It combines the statements and optimizes them so that, at the end, one large query is run which has ideally been compiled into a high-performing statement. This enables the author of SQL statements to design easily readable code or views while not having to constantly think about performance. However, be aware that this will not always work, and testing with PlanViz (Plan Visualization) is a mandatory task you need to perform.

PlanViz is an SAP HANA-based tool for analyzing and visualizing the performance and execution structure of queries.

SQL Engine

You can usually rely on an SQL engine to optimize code, and it offers good support for programmers. However, be aware that complex coding requires you to do the optimization yourself because, in these cases, the engine will not always be able to handle the code on its own.

2.1.3 SAP HANA Extended Application Services Advanced (XSA)

The previously-mentioned XS engine has undergone a change with Service Pack 11 and is now known as the XSA engine. The "A" in the XSA stands for "advanced", and means that the XS engine has now completely switched its code basis and also changed ownership within SAP. Previously, the XS engine only supported JavaScript coding and oData (a data exchange protocol developed by Microsoft). The XS engine could therefore be seen as a lightweight webserver. With the switch to XSA, node.js, Java and C++ coding are now also supported. In this way, the SAP HANA platform has been enhanced and has made the XSA engine a more heavyweight webserver.

SAP HANA 2 BYOL

With SAP HANA 2, the XSA engine now includes the option to Bring Your Own Language (BYOL), which essentially means that any coding is supported. So far, we have not seen that in action, so further testing is required.

Figure 2.2 depicts the XSA engine and its surrounding components. As the figure shows, the main components necessary to build a web application are as follows:

- A **database** is needed to store data and to execute changes to the data as requested by the application.
- The **web application** itself needs to be coded. This can be done in any language supplied by the XSA engine. Another possibility involves connecting a different webserver and using HANA only as the database.
- The third and final component is the **presentation logic**. The borders between control flow and presentation can be very fluid; for example, if you decide to build the web page using traditional client-side JavaScript (XSJS) and SAPUI5, then the code is executed on the client side and only the data exchange between client and server is handled via oData services. A second option consists of only using input from the client side, creating the webpage in HTML5 code, and implementing the more complex application logic on the server side.

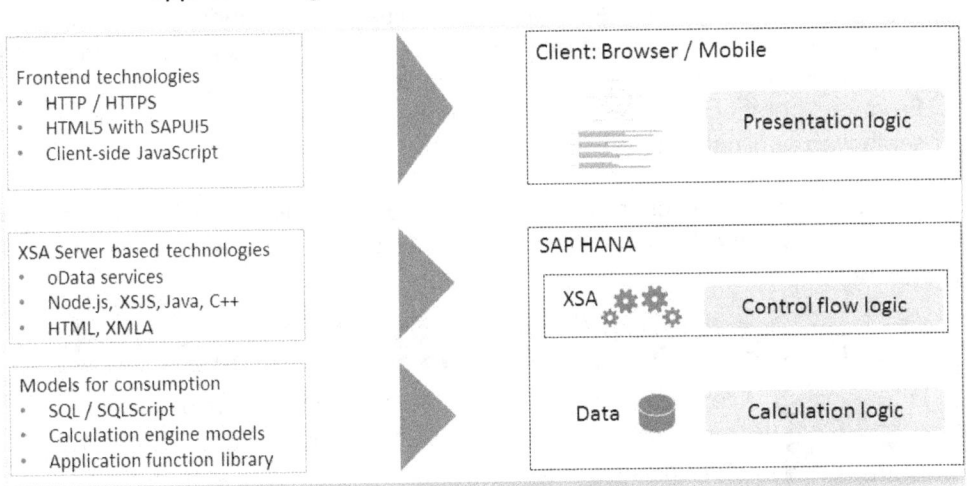

Figure 2.2: The SAP HANA XSA architecture foundation

More than just a webserver, the XSA engine is also responsible for rendering the SAP HANA Web modeling workbench. Not only are web-modeling environments for SDI or SAP HANA views run on the XSA engine, but the XSA engine also serves as an interface. It serves as the communication between the actual code execution on the database and the reports generated by the SAP HANA XS scheduler or in the web-based workbench.

Overall, the XSA engine offers a broad range of functionalities to the end user and can be seen as the main platform for any future generation developments by SAP for web-based applications. It is a comprehensive tool for building any SAP-based web applications for your company. The main language used for coding is JavaScript, although other languages are also supported. Two SAP front-end tools use SAPUI5 as a basis for implementing reports or transactions, namely SAP Fiori and SAP Design Studio. In turn, SAPUI5 is based on JavaScript and HTML5 libraries, which then deliver all the necessary functions in order to easily use charts, or form elements (e.g. input fields, tables etc.).

The XSA engine relies very heavily on JavaScript, which is one of its biggest weaknesses. JavaScript was originally designed as a lightweight alternative to Java and could be easily used for client-side code execution and simple functionalities. This included operations such as *OnClick* (when you click on a text or a picture) or *OnMouseOver* (when you move your mouse over an element), but it was initially not intended for use in complex logic. This changed over time and now there is a large community supporting node.js as an alternative to Java as a web language. From our perspective, however, the language is still not ready for large-scale web applications.

It is our belief that for large web applications popular web languages such as Java and PHP remain better-suited for server-side code development.

> **Use of the XSA engine**
>
> We recommend using the XSA engine in custom developments for small web sites, such as input forms or small web reports.
>
> We also recommend it for smaller internal reporting sites you might want to build because SAPUI5, together with the XSA engine, clearly represents the foundation for all future SAP developments.

2.1.4 SAP HANA deployment infrastructure

With SAP HANA SP 11, the SAP HANA deployment infrastructure (HDI) has been introduced in a beta version, and was only recommended for productive application development starting with Service Pack 12. It essentially changes the whole development approach in SAP HANA and bases everything on the cloud foundry approach, an industry standard for cloud applications. This means that any application developed in SAP HANA is now also portable to the cloud, with minimal effort. Of course, there is a wide range of features that have to be provided by a platform in order to comply with the cloud foundry framework. Most of these features are delivered directly with the SAP HANA platform; however, some need to be customized by the development team responsible for an application.

One of these features is the concept of the SAP HANA deployment infrastructure. The SAP HANA deployment infrastructure provides containers which need to be used in order to develop an application; however, this only applies to database objects. Any client-side JavaScript code and oData service is still activated in the usual way. A significant change is that, within this container, all SAP HANA objects required to run an application are now created with container-specific schemas. Information that used to be shared across developments is now specifically stored within the schemas of a container (e.g. metadata for views or stored procedures).

This has two main impacts:

- ▶ **Security impacts:** Security is much better than in previous applications because the applications are separate from one another (at least if the containers are used as intended). This is due to a strict segregation of applications resulting in separate access to applications. This also means that, across applications, privileges cannot be reused as easily as before.

- ▶ **Decentralization:** Because applications are now segregated, some metadata is now in decentralized storage. On one hand, this can be helpful because administrators might not have to search through endless lines in tables to find specific objects. On the other hand, this can have a negative effect if administrators need to search longer for root causes, especially when the root cause is due to the parallel actions of two applications.

Furthermore, the containers can separate design time and runtime. The design-time container lets the user define which database object types (e.g. procedures, tables, etc.), in which database version (e.g. Service Pack 11), should be included in a deployment scenario. The defined database version is backward compatible, meaning that if objects were developed in a later Service Pack, they could still be deployed in the Service Pack 11 environment, but not the other way around.

The runtime container lets the developer specify the syntax for naming the runtime objects created.

> **Example of a runtime naming convention**
>
>
> An application is named *ExampleApp*, the procedure file is called *ExProc* and the subfolder in which this application is stored is named *ProcFolder*. The namespace file can then define whether the runtime object will be generated as: *ExampleApp.ProcFolder::ExProc* or as *ExampleApp::ExProc*

All in all, it makes sense to use containers in structuring new developments. This has been a trend in other recent development environments. In addition, it makes the deployment of applications easier. However, any issues in design objects can lead to problems in deployment. This can be particularly problematic if several developers are working in parallel on one container.

> **HANA deployment infrastructure**
>
>
> The HANA deployment infrastructure makes SAP HANA database applications much more secure. Therefore, we recommend using HDI for any future developments. For a very good example of HDI works, please visit the following webpage:
>
> *https://blogs.sap.com/2015/12/08/sap-hana-sps-11-new-developer-features-hdi/*

2.1.5 SAP HANA views

SAP HANA views are one of the many innovations that come with the platform. They deliver an easy way to merge data from several tables and to perform operations on this data. They mainly rely on drag and drop modeling, especially with calculation views. So, let's look first at the history and development of these views.

The construct foundation of SAP HANA views has changed dramatically with the SAP HANA platform developments over the last few years. SAP started out with attribute, analytical and calculation views. In our previous book *SAP HANA Advanced Modeling,* we recommended only using calculation views, but this endorsement of calculation views has changed with the latest releases.

SAP S/4HANA has been the more recent focus of SAP's development with regard to ERP and operations. Due to the new strategic orientation, changes can be found in the way SAP HANA views should be modeled and used going forward. One of these changes is the predicted removal of attribute and analytical views from SAP's modeling environment with the HANA deployment infrastructure (see Section 2.1.4). More surprising is the elimination of scripted calculation views, which have now been replaced with SQLScript functions. In itself, this does not represent any functionality change, but it does show the general orientation of SAP towards a more SQL-based modeling in the entire SAP HANA database.

Furthermore, with SAP S/4HANA, SAP pushes the use of CDS views, and HDI itself only leverages CDS built table structures; this again underlines the move towards a more code-oriented infrastructure

Figure 2.3 shows the change in the modeling of SAP HANA views from earlier versions to the latest releases.

This change in optimal modeling highlights the difficulties for SAP customers when deciding on the correct path for future applications. However, for agile developments and an easy combination of data for testing purposes, we still believe that SAP HANA views are the best option.

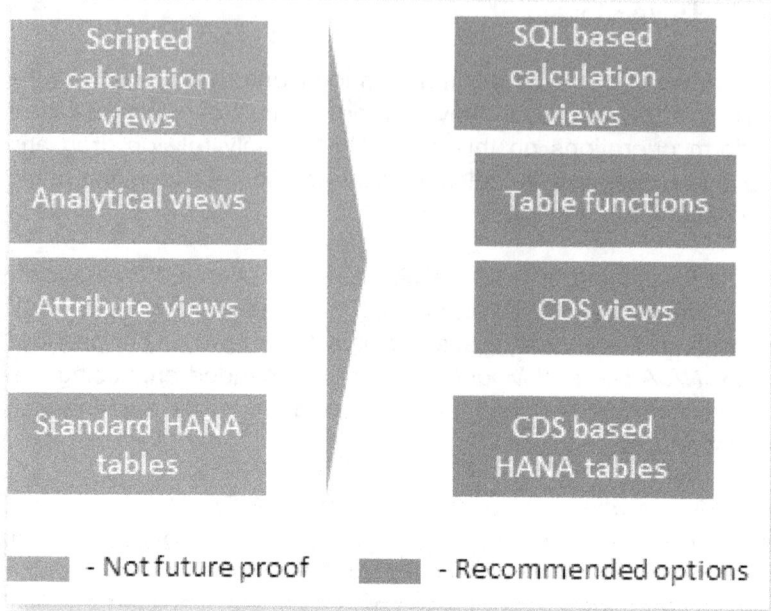

Figure 2.3: Change in SAP HANA modeling

Calculation views in particular currently offer a vast range of out-of-the-box functionalities for an effective realization of business value. The drag and drop interface lets a developer quickly assemble all necessary data in order to achieve the desired output. Among the functionality offered for structuring and merging data, these views offer aggregations, projections, filters, rankings, unions, and many other common functions.

The Core Data Services (CDS) views offer SQL syntax in an SAP HANA integrated manner. This means that a view is constructed with the typical SELECT...FROM...WHERE syntax (and additional standard SQL syntax), but is integrated into a CDS document. The only difference to other databases is that the format, in which the code is written, alters slightly and that the view is called CDS view and not simply SQL view.

Additionally, CDS (as part of CDS documents) offers the language to construct tables, associations (or referential integrity rules), namespaces, etc. Seen as a whole, CDS is a large SQL-based language with which database structures can be handled in a manner specific to SAP HANA.

> **SAP HANA views recommendation**
>
>  We recommend the use of SAP HANA views for rapid developments and quick insights. Refrain from using them for large, long-term data warehouse developments. CDS seems to be the strategic way forward. We recommend reading the developer guide for further insight into this technology:
>
> http://help.sap.com/hana/SAP_HANA_Core_Data_Services_CDS_Reference_en.pdf

2.1.6 SAP HANA libraries and functionalities

This section covers libraries and further functionalities that are relevant for building a comprehensive SAP HANA BI architecture.

SAP HANA libraries

The SAP HANA libraries represent a set of prebuilt functions that can be executed via a function or procedure call. The libraries supplied with SAP HANA are: the business function library (BFL), the application function library (AFL), and the predictive analysis library (PAL). Additionally, it is possible to program your own function modules or libraries with C++. Although these libraries are delivered out-of-the-box, they must be installed separately.

The predictive analysis library will be detailed in Section 2.4. In our experience, BFL and AFL are rarely used in productive environments within companies, which indicates that these libraries do not deliver much value to the customer. Why is that? First of all, they require a specific input format including separate tables. Secondly, these functions represent standard processes and do not take into account customer specifics.

SAP HANA spatial

There are further interesting elements of the SAP HANA platform that require discussion; for example, the SAP HANA spatial engine. This engine is necessary for analyzing geographic data and depicting geographic charts. One of the most common uses for these reports is to provide a view of the area generating the highest sales volume. A more futuristic analysis could involve identifying areas which will most likely be hit by a catastrophe (e.g., for insurance companies). In order to perform spatial analysis of any kind, the SAP HANA spatial engine delivers the required functionality. With SP 12 in particular, the spatial engine has evolved to include more generic geographic data formats.

SAP HANA text analysis

Another well-known functionality is SAP HANA text analysis. This feature offers text analysis and can identify whether an author has referred to something positively or negatively.

Example of the text analysis feature in SAP HANA

Imagine a questionnaire in which the participants are asked in free text form if they would like to make any further suggestions; someone answers with: "I do not like your product A". Using SAP HANA text analysis, an evaluation of all the free text comments given from that questionnaire would then return a result that at least one negative comment was made about product A.

The text analysis can be applied to many situations, the most relevant being the assessment of social media data. Nonetheless, the same data can be obtained by purchasing aggregated and analyzed data from social media analytics platforms. Because these platforms already investigate such a huge amount of data, and provide factual results, there is no question that buying the data from these companies could be much more profitable.

However, there are smaller cases where evaluating questionnaires or an internal social media platform can be handled via SAP HANA, and it makes sense to use the text analysis feature.

> **SAP HANA core functionalities**
>
>  PAL and the SAP HANA spatial engine deliver great value to the platform, whereas BFL and AFL have seen little utilization in companies so far. In general, with these libraries and functionalities, we recommend assessing the value to your company in using them.

2.2 SAP S/4HANA Embedded Analytics

In this section, we introduce you to the recent quantum leap in the SAP ERP world. We highlight significant changes that have taken place to the former SAP ECC stack and what important pillars SAP S/4HANA and SAP S/4HANA Embedded Analytics represent today. In addition, these developments have not failed to leave their mark on the design of a sustainable and modern BI architecture. A common theme throughout this book is the consideration of this impact. Looking at our reference architecture, the data generation and data digestion and storage layers encompass artifacts of SAP S/4HANA and SAP S/4HANA Embedded Analytics.

2.2.1 SAP S/4HANA

With SAP S/4HANA (data generation layer) the next generation of business suite has entered the market, bringing with it a complete redesign of its architecture and data models in order to leverage the features and capabilities of SAP HANA. With the Simple Finance enhancement in 2014, SAP presented the first step into a new era driven by the "simple" paradigm. Agility, flexibility and simplicity in business processes became the motto of SAP's ERP applications, running and benefitting from the in-memory SAP HANA platform. The key rationale for the introduction of Simple Finance was the instant financial insights obtained without the need for duplication or aggregation of data, thereby acting as a single version of truth. However, the Simple Finance enhancement builds on the SAP ERP 6.0 stack and the launch of SAP S/4HANA resulted in a completely new codebase and data model. SAP S/4HANA demonstrates SAP's direction toward one database, one platform, and one system.

Today, SAP S/4HANA Finance is the best choice when it comes to implementing new, future-oriented finance solutions (in an SAP environment). However, not only did finance applications evolve and transform to conform to the "new world", other lines of business (LOB) are also about to pass, or already have passed, a similar metamorphosis to a completely new setup based on SAP HANA (e.g. Logistics).

In summarizing the changes coming with SAP S/4HANA, we would like to emphasize the following elements:

- **New architecture and data models**: SAP S/4HANA constitutes a complete redesign towards optimized architecture and data models running on the SAP HANA database. This re-architecting focusses on leveraging in-memory capabilities through code push down, data compression, and OLAP + Online Transaction Processing (OLTP) merge. The simplified data model aims to eliminate data redundancies, to clearly segregate master and transactional data, and to accelerate processes. Aggregates and indices are concepts of the past and have been removed in order to achieve greater flexibility and data throughput by reducing the data/memory footprints in SAP HANA. From a functional perspective, project experiences from the last decades were compiled to form the blueprint of SAP S/4HANA Enterprise Management, which is today the digital core for LOB solutions such as finance, logistics, manufacturing, and supply chain.

- **Renewed applications and frontend**: Building on the new data structures, applications and transactions have improved through new features and self-service capabilities, better runtime, and a completely new look and feel. Additionally, the real-time capability of SAP S/4HANA offers instant insights and individual analyses. Planning, prediction, and simulations at the highest level of granularity are now possible. SAP Fiori Apps support these features and build the new state-of-the-art frontend for entering personalized work and transaction lists. Technologically, SAP Fiori is enabled by HTML5 and SAPUI5 which can also be used on various (mobile) devices. SAP S/4HANA integrates and interacts closely with SAP partner solutions such as SuccessFactors, Ariba, and Fieldglass, providing a variety of opportunities to tailor and enhance your SAP S/4HANA implementation to your specific demands.

- **Cloud or on-premise**: SAP S/4HANA offers not only an on-premise delivery model, but is also available in the cloud. The cloud edition might be the right choice for customers looking for a lightweight model, with the option to easily scale their solution. Customers can choose a public and a private offering, but both come with standardized packages with customization restrictions. The on-premise solution enables full customization because the entire installation runs under full-control of the owner. The on-premise deployment can be executed through a variety of hosting models including partner-managed private clouds. Nonetheless, an in-between option is to choose a hybrid model. Section 2.6 covers cloud platforms in more detail.

In Figure 2.4 we show the key lines of business and their associated partner solutions.

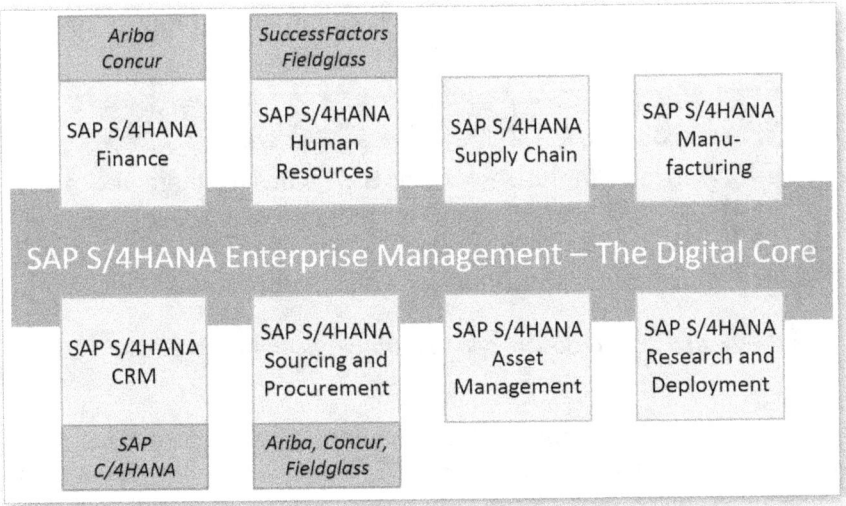

Figure 2.4: Overview of SAP S/4HANA lines of business

Let's have a closer look at what has changed in the major lines of business such as finance or logistics. Each LOB comprises a set of solutions in its specific domain; for example, for SAP S/4HANA Finance, there is financial planning analysis, accounting and financial closing, treasury and financial risk management). The key modification for the aforementioned LOBs is a completely rearranged data model. While in earlier ERP versions, duplicate data sets existed, in the new SAP S/4HANA system there is only one universal table and truth. In finance, the ACDOCA and logistics MATDOC tables represent the central objects for the applications. ACDOCA, for instance, incorporates both the finance and controlling view, enabling data analyses from different angles without costly pre-calculations and combinations of dozens of tables. From a business perspective, the simplification of the data model is easily recognizable. In the logistics module, business objects are now merged and are available as one (e. g. shopping cart and purchase requisition). Additionally, business processes are streamlined and optimized (e. g. Procurement to Pay, Order to Cash). Finally, fewer user interaction steps are needed to obtain specific information or to complete a transaction, which in turn reduces reaction time and increases flexibility in your daily business.

For your journey to SAP S/4HANA, SAP has introduced SAP Activate, which represents an innovation adaption framework. SAP Activate provides methodology and tools to support your deployment plan, and offers a non-disruptive migration path. Throughout the entire product lifecycle, SAP Activate can expedite your implementation.

SAP S/4HANA—further information

In addition to the actual SAP website, there are many locations where you can obtain insights into SAP S/4. However, we recommend using the official community website for questions and discussions:

https://www.sap.com/products/s4hana-erp-cloud/community.html.

From our point of view, SAP S/4HANA offers great opportunities to accelerate and streamline both your SAP ERP landscape and the supported business processes. However, please keep in mind that SAP S/4HANA is only a young product and there is still not much experience in big migrations (they are ongoing). Moreover, you should be prepared to re-think fundamentals in comparing business processes (e.g., thoughts on cost-based versus account-based Cost and Profit Analysis (COPA)). Looking at the technology and our core topic of SAP HANA BI architectures, of particular importance are: changes in the source adapters for data extraction (e.g. adaption of standard extractors to new SAP S/4HANA structures, switch to CDS views), the right architectural spot for preparing reporting and analytics, the utilization of the embedded

SAP BW, and the interplay between the SAP HANA platforms (or is just one common SAP HANA platform the right solution?). These topics will accompany us throughout this book.

2.2.2 SAP S/4HANA Embedded Analytics

While introducing SAP S/4HANA, we mentioned the merge of OLTP and OLAP utilizing the features of SAP HANA. This leads to the good old question of the separation of transactional and analytical reporting (and the assignment to a layer in our reference architecture). Interestingly, we are faced with this question in almost every SAP HANA project when it comes to any kind of reporting. SAP offers a solution for operational reporting and has introduced **SAP S/4HANA Embedded Analytics**. This component contains analytics features integrated into the SAP S/4HANA suite. It enables business users to execute real-time reports and analyses based on live transactional data. Furthermore, these analytical features are part of the SAP S/4HANA distribution, and are directly useable. SAP S/4HANA Embedded Analytics comes with pre-defined, out-of-the-box views of the transactional data. Virtual Data Model (VDM) is the new key word for business users to gain desired insights and information within the transactional SAP S/4HANA system. These default solutions are enriched by ready-to-deploy best practice solution packages. Formerly known as Rapid Deployment Solution (RDS), SAP renamed its portfolio of analytical content to SAP Best Practices for analytics with SAP S/4HANA. Additionally, there are guidelines available on how best to integrate SAP S/4HANA Embedded Analytics with existing or traditional platforms, for reporting and analytics (e.g. SAP Business Objects, SAP BW, SAP HANA Cloud Platform). In addition to the SAP guidelines, we tackle these architectural challenges in subsequent chapters of this book.

> **SAP S/4HANA Embedded Analytics—further information**
>
>  A comprehensive guide and explanation of SAP S/4HANA Embedded Analytics is provided at:
>
> *https://blogs.sap.com/2016/03/10/sap-s4hana-embedded-analytics-a-detailed-walkthrough-part-13/*. Furthermore, we recommend identifying best practice solutions for your specific scenario by visiting the following SAP website: *https://rapid.sap.com/bp/BP_S4H_ANA* (authorization required).

At this point, in addressing the initial question of distinguishing operational and analytical reporting, we characterize only the SAP S/4HANA Embedded Analytics component itself. Discussions and recommendations of any combination, interplay, or integration with other tools and technologies offering analytical features are covered in Chapter 3. From our experience, SAP S/4HANA Embedded Analytics is positioned as a built-in component of SAP S/4HANA for running reports and analyses on operational data (also in real-time). It offers a lightweight modeling and data model consumption featuring CDS view technology (for further information on CDS views, see Section 2.1.5). The out -of-the-box CDS views can be enhanced via individual programming and reused in various scenarios. As a starting point, the predefined VDMs cover the most relevant use cases to bring SAP S/4HANA Embedded Analytics into action (e.g. via factsheets and search functionality).

In relation to this book's key question, we consider SAP S/4HANA Embedded Analytics to be an important part of the holistic discussion of a modern, performant, and sustainable reporting solution and handle it as part of the data digestion and storage layer.

2.3 SAP BW/4HANA

Since the first launch of SAP BW about 20 years ago, the product has undergone several stages of evolution. One of the most troublesome aspects of this product was the performance of developed applications. To mitigate this issue, SAP has introduced step-wise, in-memory-based components and features: first, the introduction of the SAP BW Accelerator in release 7.0; then, the introduction of SAP HANA as the technical database for SAP BW (SAP BW 7.3, SP 5); and finally ,the latest release known as SAP BW/4HANA which is thoroughly aligned to SAP HANA. In its core, SAP BW/4HANA is considered a member of the data digestion and storage layer.

Before we dive into the changes and features, which are delivered with SAP BW/4HANA, let's first have a closer look at what this release represents: SAP promotes SAP BW/4HANA as a logical continuation of the previous SAP BW versions, leading to the next generation of the SAP data warehouse platform. Nevertheless, the foundation and SAP BW modeling principles remain the same. However, the new SAP BW/4HANA product is built on a new innovation code line, which is not only optimized for SAP HANA, but also runs only on SAP HANA. Like other vendors, SAP obviously took a strategic decision towards supporting only one database product (their own). A rationale for this is certainly the concentration of all product development efforts into SAP's simplification roadmap by integrating and optimizing all their SAP HANA products towards one database, one platform, and one system.

> **What is SAP BW/4HANA—overview**
>
>  A good summary of the key innovations and changes which come with SAP BW/4HANA can be found in the following blog:
>
> *https://blogs.saphana.com/2016/08/31/what-is-bw4hana/.*

So, what are the key differentiators and improvements of SAP BW/4HANA? Moreover, what does a radically-optimized SAP HANA release mean? We outline our point of view on this new, major release below:

- **Data modeling objects**—With each of the earlier SAP BW editions, SAP continued to support obsolete data modelling concepts from previous versions (e.g. SAP BW 3.5 transfer rules in SAP BW 7.x). SAP BW/4HANA has now broken this rule by terminating the support of many old concepts and object types. For the design of an SAP BW/4HANA data model, only four selected object types are accepted, which are optimized for use with SAP HANA without any burdens from the past. InfoObjects and Advanced DataStore Objects (ADSOs) represent the persistency layer, and Open ODS view and CompositeProvider represent the virtual layer. Figure 2.5 gives an overview of the conversion from the historical object types to the new ones.

39

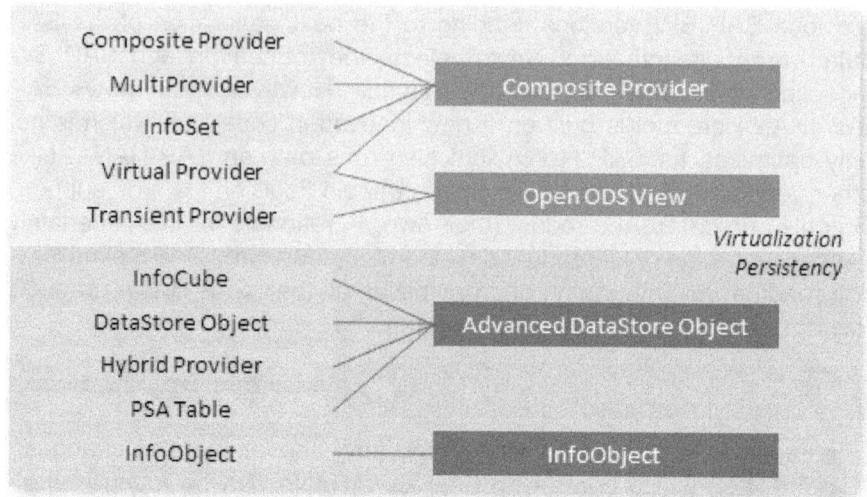

Figure 2.5: SAP BW/4HANA data modeling object types (source SAP)

- **Data modeling principles**—The LSA++ architecture, as SAP's principal design guideline, remains the same. The key to a modern BI architecture is the right balance of persistency and virtualization. SAP BW/4HANA strictly follows the idea of having less persistent layers leading to a lean and flexible data model. Less object types for data modeling, together with fewer persistency layers, increase the consistency within, and of, your data model. In short, you spend less effort and experience fewer errors while implementing, adjusting, and running your SAP BW/4HANA application.

SAP HANA LSA++ architecture

 A complete documentation and explanation of the LSA++ approach can be found at:

https://help.sap.com/saphelp_nw74/helpdata/en/22/ad6fad96b547c199adb588107e6412/frameset.htm

- **Data modeling tools**—A graphical data flow modeling tool is provided. Key functionalities are available to enable design using drag-and-drop, and to visualize the flow of your data end-to-end, resulting in increased transparency from the SAP BW Data-

Source to any architected data mart. You can also navigate directly to the editor pane of each object. The Graphical data flow modeler is dispatched with the Eclipse environment.

- **Strong integration with SAP HANA**—Another central and established element of SAP BW/4HANA is the push down of calculation processes to where the data resides. OLAP, Planning, and data management operations can be increasingly handled by the engines of SAP HANA. Earlier ABAP Managed Database Procedures (AMDP) also need to be mentioned in this context. Additionally, with SAP BW/4HANA, the focus has been extended to bring SAP HANA's technical possibilities to SAP BW. Some of the key concepts include SAP HANA native views, which are incorporated in an SAP BW managed data model (i.e. hybrid data model approach utilizing CompositeProvider or Open ODS views), and SAP HANA Analysis Processes which, for example, access libraries for predictive analytics or business rules. A combination of these, or another self-reliant approach, is the creation of custom SAP HANA native views on top of automatically-generated calculation views of SAP BW objects, which are used directly by SAP BusinessObjects Cloud, Lumira, certified 3rd party tools, or which lead back to SAP BW. This works for Queries, CompositeProviders, ADSOs, and InfoObjects and opens your SAP BW application to any custom (SQL) enhancement needed. From our perspective, the interplay between SAP BW/4HANA and SAP HANA native creates the highest number of challenges for architects. We revisit this discussion in Section 3.7.

SAP BW/4HANA and SAP HANA native—foundation

The advantages of a managed SAP BW versus a freestyle SAP HANA native data warehouse are detailed in the following blog:

https://blogs.saphana.com/2014/07/28/data-warehousing-on-hana-managed-or-freestyle-bw-or-native/.

- **Smart data lifecycle management**—SAP BW/4HANA is now capable of automatically supporting dynamic tiering. This means that by analyzing the metadata relating to type and location of data (location refers to the corresponding table), SAP

BW/4HANA can determine the assignment of data to hot and warm regions. The utilization of hardware resources is therefore improved. For ADSOs, dynamic tiering settings can now be maintained at object and partition level via the object's editor. A new way of handling warm data was introduced in 2016: *SAP HANA Extension Nodes*. Leveraging scale-out architectures, these kinds of server nodes allow an overload of their storage capacity (compared to regular SAP HANA slave nodes). SAP BW/4HANA customers benefit from lower scale-out environment costs because fewer nodes and less overall RAM are needed, but the same amount of data can still be handled. However, the impact on backup and recovery times needs to be kept in mind.

SAP HANA Extension Nodes—further details

Further details about SAP HANA Extension Nodes are provided in the following blog:

https://blogs.sap.com/2016/04/26/more-details-hana-extension-nodes-for-bw-on-hana/.

- ▸ **Cloud or on-premise**—What do you prefer? There is no easy answer, but now a new option has been introduced for SAP BW customers to deploy their solution. SAP provides not only their SAP HANA Enterprise Cloud (HEC) but also Amazon Web Services (AWS) and Microsoft Azure. This is another key area we will concentrate on in Section 2.8 because there are many questions and advisory needs in choosing the right, or right mix of, deployment approach(es). From our experience, this is not only about costs, functionality, and data security, but also needs a holistic governance to manage all pieces and facets of your current and future SAP BW landscape. So, take your time to understand and find the right approach for your specific scenario.

- ▸ **Modern user interface**—In recent releases, we have seen data modeling features in SAP GUI and SAP HANA Studio mutually complementing each other. For example, the definition of a CompositeProvider happens in SAP HANA Studio only, but process chains are managed in the SAP GUI. Therefore, the respective SAP BW Modeling Plugin is essential for SAP HANA Studio. SAP BW/4HANA continues in this direction and also considers the new Web Development Workbench (Web IDE). The latter is becoming increasingly important for administering and working with SAP HANA, and thus, also with SAP BW/4HANA. For end-user reporting and for analysis requirements, both the BusinessObjects Cloud and the traditional SAP Business Objects suite are supported.

Installation of SAP BW/4HANA modeling tools

Details about installing and accessing the necessary SAP BW/4HANA modeling tools in SAP HANA Studio are provided at:

http://help.sap.com/download/netweaver/bwmt/SAP_BW_Modeling_Tools_Installation_Guide_en.pdf

- **Migration**—SAP supports its customers with a migration path to SAP BW/4HANA. The SAP BW/4HANA Starter AddOn comprises of tools for migration. However, as of today, there are some prerequisites to consider when entering the new world. First, you have to be using only SAP HANA-optimized objects, as well as only Operational Data Provisioning (ODP), Flat file, or SAP HANA source systems. Additionally, you need to eliminate your 3.x data flow and BEx front-end tools. Nearline Storage (NLS) partner solutions are also not possible when moving to SAP BW/4HANA. Therefore, with your SAP BW system, powered by SAP HANA, you have to carefully consider the SAP BW/4HANA specifications before the Starter AddOn can help you to convert your system. Nevertheless, SAP's automated conversion and migration tools have worked quite well in the past. From our project experience, the functionality is mostly transferred correctly, but we have realized that the new setup of a migrated transformation or ABAP is often not optimal. Adjustments and maintenance of migrated objects have sometimes been messy. Therefore, be careful when using the migration/transfer tool and after the first dry run, check the quality of the outcome by doing more than just confirming the accuracy of a query result.

> **The migration path to SAP BW/4HANA**
>
>
> A good overview of the path to SAP BW/4HANA is outlined in the following blog:
>
> *https://blogs.saphana.com/2016/09/07/the-road-to-sap-bw4hana-part-1/*.

▶ **Data integration**—The way to integrate data from various sources is now simplified and streamlined into two approaches: *SAP HANA source system* for non-SAP sources and the *ODP source system* framework for all SAP-based (ABAP) systems. The former builds on SAP HANA platform capabilities represented by the SAP Enterprise Information Management (EIM) component; in this case, SAP *Smart Data Integration* (SDI). SDI was previously introduced and integrated into SAP HANA as a "lightweight version" of the Data Services tool and enables graphical design of data transformations in SAP HANA Studio. Today, and with SAP HANA 2, the functionality and the available adapters of the SAP HANA platform have grown. In an SAP BW/4HANA scenario, SDI acts as mediator between various non-SAP source systems, making direct access and real-time replication possible. Data provisioning via SDI is executed on the SAP HANA side. Looking at the ODP framework, this is now the only option to connect to SAP ABAP-based source systems such as SAP ECC or SAP S/4HANA. The Operational Delta Queue (ODQ) takes on the delta handling. ODP can handle data extraction sourced on CDS views, SAP HANA views, SAP ERP extractors, and SLT. Data consumers can be SAP BW, SAP S/4HANA Embedded Analytics, SAP Data Services, and OData Sources. Installing and changing your existing source systems to the ODP framework will require a disproportionate effort at your end because, after the migration, there will only be a source system and no further transformations. This results in many rounds of testing, but getting rid of the multiple connection types will be worth it. Figure 2.6 illustrates the new way to connect sources to SAP BW.

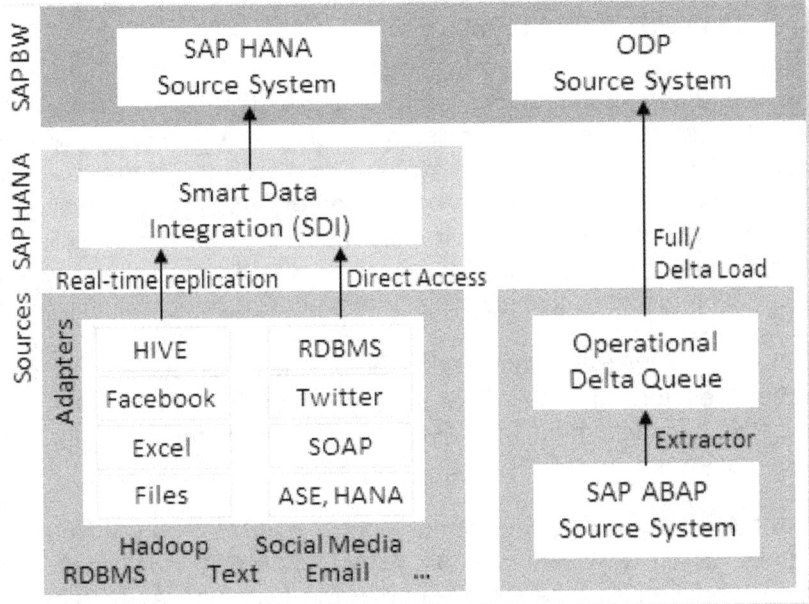

Figure 2.6: Data integration options in SAP BW/4HANA (source SAP)

With SAP BW/4HANA, support of planning functions based on *Integrated Planning* (IP) with *Planning Application Kit* (PAK) or *Business Planning and Consolidation* (BPC) has been announced by SAP, but has not yet been implemented. Further enhancements will be released as part of Feature Packs providing optimized Business Content, further Cloud integrations and extended interplay with Hadoop.

SAP has taken an important step toward a flexible and future-oriented positioning of SAP BW/4HANA by cutting crucial ties to the past. Looking at current SAP BW implementations and many half-hearted approaches to leveraging the power of SAP HANA in SAP BW, we are convinced that it was a necessary step to support only SAP HANA-optimized objects. This is crucial in order to build your SAP BW data warehouse and keep it up to date with innovative, volatile, and highly-demanding analysis requirements that can pop up from anywhere, at any time.

2.4 Data provisioning tools

When SAP BW was introduced, and for a long time after, SAP's only strategy for data provisioning consisted of using ABAP-coded extractors to acquire data from SAP source systems and then transform the data itself in SAP BW. Extractors could be created or enhanced in the source system by ABAP developers, and transformations performed in SAP BW had to be coded mostly in ABAP as well. This was because the standard transformation functionality only allowed for very simple operations.

That changed with SAP's acquisition of BusinessObjects and its ETL Data Services tool in 2007. Over the years, SAP gradually adopted graphical ETL modeling, not in SAP BW, but as a general integration into their tool repertoire.

SAP HANA is the main subject of this book. Therefore, we will focus on SAP tools, which work well with SAP HANA/SAP BW. Additionally, we will take a brief look at the most common Big Data ETL and streaming tools.

Figure 2.7 shows a simplified overview of the tools discussed in this chapter. The only exceptions are the SAP BW HANA source system and ODP extraction, which were presented in Section 2.3.

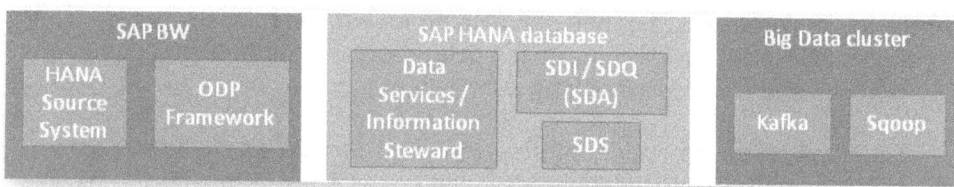

Figure 2.7: Data provisioning tools discussed in Chapter 2

Before going into the details of these tools, we need to differentiate between *ETL/ELT* tools and streaming technology. Going forward we use the term ETL synonymously for both ELT and ETL; it is only the order in which tasks are executed that differentiates these two concepts, but the tasks themselves are the same.

ETL can be defined as: extraction of data from one or several sources (E), transformation of the data in order to harmonize and cleanse the data (T), and finally, loading of the data into the target (L). These activities are typically completed in batches, and either take existing data for lookups, or merge the data from different tables. There are also real-time ETL processes, but they are usually only near real-time because it might take several minutes to adjust the data to the target format and perform the actual insertion.

In contrast to ETL, data streaming has only developed in recent years with the creation of Big Data clusters and the rise of large in-memory calculations. Streaming technology is used for large amounts of data which need to be processed in real-time. Streaming is typically used for sensor data or social media platforms. Therefore, the number of transformation tasks has to be kept to an absolute minimum. When doing lookups, for example, the number of records kept in memory should be kept to a minimum, and should generally only reflect a limited period of time (e.g. data from the last three seconds). The challenge for streaming tools lies in ensuring that all data is transferred completely and, in the case of data loss (e.g. it cannot be processed in real-time due to limited resources), in minimizing the amount of data lost.

Data provisioning tools can encompass all three layers of our reference architecture—data generation, data digestion and storage, and data consumption.

2.4.1 ETL tools

In this section, we look at SAP Data Services, Information Steward, SDI/SDQ, and Sqoop.

SAP Data Services

SAP Data Services delivers ETL functionality such as **jobs, workflows** and **data flows**. These are managed in a graphical user interface and data flows are mostly modeled graphically.

Jobs can be scheduled to run in certain time intervals and are monitored via a cockpit in SAP Data Services. There are standard parameters that are monitored, but usually the developer adds certain additional information to the data load and writes it to a table, which can then be integrated into the monitoring cockpit in the form of a report. The information stored in additional tables includes the number of rows which had to be cleansed, or how many rows were extracted and/or inserted.

The next levels down are **workflows**. Workflows are used to group data flows into functionally or technically similar units.

> ### Data flow grouping into workflows
>
>  When a company needs to load all the data for the finance department, for example, the SAP Data Services developer splits these flows into manageable parts in order to keep track of all the transformations. Once all the data flows have been modeled, they can then be combined in a sequential order in the workflow.

Finally, the lowest levels are **data flows,** which then contain the actual transformations of the data. Data flows start with the selection of data from at least one table and end with the insertion, update or upsert of one or several data targets (e.g. tables, files).

SAP Data Services offers default data transformations such as merge, union, aggregation, ranking, various calculation options and many more. Additionally, there is a data quality component, which enables the use of algorithms for improving data quality. This part of Data services can help in cleaning up addresses or adding geographical information.

From our experience, the possibilities offered graphically in the data flows are sufficient to cover almost every scenario. It is rarely required to script code, except when having to change or read variables necessary for the execution of the data flow.

SAP Data Services is now very closely integrated with SAP HANA. When using SAP HANA as a database for the execution of data flows, SAP Data Services translates most transformation types into SQL code and executes the code on the SAP HANA database, thereby leveraging the calculation power of SAP HANA.

Building Blocks of an SAP HANA Architecture

> **Positioning of SAP Data Services**
>
>
>
> From our perspective, the positioning of SAP Data Services within the SAP tool suite is not completely clear. For all customers who use SAP HANA as the data target, SDI and SDQ are the recommended solutions (we explain in more detail later in this chapter). However, SAP Data Services also provides functionality that is not yet available in SDI/SDQ. So, before deciding on one tool or the other, we recommend first checking your requirements and latest SAP product updates.

SAP Information Steward

The SAP Information Steward is an add-on for SAP Data Services and enables business users to easily check data quality and implement business rules. These business rules can be tested before developers integrate them into SAP Data Services. In large analytics projects in particular, business users are only able to check the quality and accuracy of transformed data at a very late stage. This is because data first has to be extracted and transformed before business value is generated. By the time business users finally get to see the data, it might be very costly to correct any errors. At this point, Information Steward comes in. The tool enables a closer cooperation between IT and business during the development process.

Smart Data Integration and Smart Data Quality

SAP recommends using Smart Data Integration (SDI) and Smart Data Quality (SDQ) when using SAP HANA tables as a target for an ETL process. SDI and SDQ offer functionality similar to SAP Data Services, including a graphical, web-based modeling environment, which runs on the XS/XSA engine.

Figure 2.8 gives a general overview of the functionality provided with SDI and SDQ, which is not as rich as with Data Services, but should cover most of your transformation needs.

49

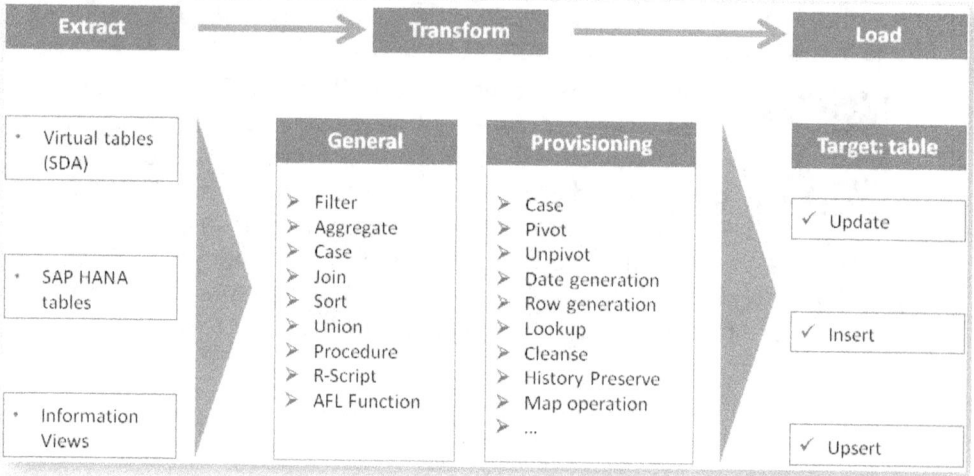

Figure 2.8: Overview of the SDI and SDQ functionality

Unfortunately, SDI and SDQ still lack the possibility to group several data flows into workflows. Furthermore, the tool is still maturing, especially because it switched to the XSA engine with SAP HANA SPS 12.

Sqoop

Sqoop is an open-source tool for data import, specifically from relational databases into Hadoop, and provides simple ETL functionalities via MapReduce. In addition, data can be exported again to be stored in relational databases. Sqoop, like most Big Data tools, is command-line based and does not offer a graphical user interface. In the current version (v1.4.6) there are not many options for data transformation tasks. Examples are the Sqoop-merge command which enables you to merge two datasets, taking into account only the latest data set for each primary key. There is also the possibility to use free-form SQL queries, but these do not allow for complex queries with subqueries or complex where clauses. Sqoop is also discussed in Section 2.7 of this book in the context of Big Data ecosystems.

> **Use of Sqoop**
>
>  Overall, we do not recommend the use of Sqoop for real ETL work, but it may make sense when importing large data sets into SAP HANA. Another possible scenario is to use Sqoop for the entry layer and store data according to their historical truths in HDFS. You can then transfer required data into the traditional data warehouse environment for any further transformations. More information about the use of Sqoop can be found in the user guide at:
>
> *https://sqoop.apache.org/docs/1.4.6/SqoopUserGuide.html.*

2.4.2 Streaming functionality

As previously explained, streaming is very different from ETL. Let us take a brief look at what functionality streams entail:

- **Source**—A source can be anything from a sensor in a machine to a social media platform or a stock market web service connector. Additionally, a typical source, such as a database, can also be connected.

- **Filters**—Filtering out data, which is unnecessary for further analysis, can be very important in order to minimize the data evaluated in-memory. Nevertheless, the full data set might be needed for further analysis, but you should still consider using only limited data for transformations.

- **Alert**—It is often necessary to check whether data exceeds a certain threshold (e.g. a machine is running too hot). In such cases, the relevant personnel need to be informed immediately in order to take action.

- **Aggregates**—It may be necessary to aggregate values in order to create a small table for storing value progression over time.

- **Merges/splits**—To execute different operations on the same data, a split of the data set can be beneficial. This also applies to merging streams or aggregates after an operation is completed.

- **Lookups/reference tables**—A value progression table, created through aggregation, can be used to check whether there is a discernible trend in the data which requires a user alert.
- **Data sink**—Because large amounts of data need to be stored, the data is usually transferred to a Big Data cluster database or a large relational database which runs on storage disks.

Different tools offer different functionality, such as joins or machine learning algorithms. Each operation needs to be handled with care, because they all take up memory space and use CPU power; and data streaming actually thrives from real-time processing. Most tools offer the possibility to ensure that no data is lost and that errors are handled consistently. If the data option is enabled so that no data is lost, then data will be stored immediately and logs will be kept, but this can result in the stream moving further and further away from real-time.

Smart Data Streaming

SAP Smart Data Streaming (SDS) is SAP's graphical tool for streaming data and has been on the market since 2014. The tool has undergone development and can now also interact with Kafka. Nevertheless, it does not offer the same set of libraries as established tools such as IBM InfoSphere Streams. The aforementioned typical tool functionality is, however, available and meets general requirements for streaming data with SAP HANA.

Apache Kafka

Apache Kafka, as Apache now calls it, is a *distributed streaming platform*. This basically means that it leverages the power of a Big Data cluster for performing streaming operations. Kafka is a very powerful tool for building streams. Programming is done using Java or Scala language. Joins, aggregates, merges, and many other processing features can be integrated via the streams API. However, be careful to keep data operations to a minimum in order to achieve your real-time goals.

> **Apache Kafka—further information**
>
>
>
> Kafka is very powerful, so we recommend reading the Kafka documentation to work out the most suitable features for your streaming scenario. The latest information about the capabilities of Kafka can be found here:
>
> *https://kafka.apache.org/documentation#streamsapi*

2.5 Analytics components

This section presents the different technologies and tools for predictive analytics based on the SAP HANA platform. Although the tools discussed here may not always be the best tools for your situation, we can say with certainty that the ones we recommend here are the ones that work best with the SAP HANA platform. At the end of this section, we briefly introduce alternative tools and why they do not work so effectively with SAP HANA.

But first, let's look at what predictive analytics entails. It can be defined as methodology that uses statistical algorithms, machine learning, and data-mining techniques in order to make predictions for the future, based on all relevant data available. The focus lies specifically on predicting future outcomes in order to deliver business value to a company.

While modeling with these tools, many important factors can be found which influence future outcomes and can be altered by a company in order to achieve a more desirable outcome. We provide an example of this below.

> **Example of a prediction**
>
>
>
> A company wants to predict the sales of cars. The sales trends of the past show that there are certain factors that positively influence the car sales: color (mostly grey and black), ease of use of the technical user interface, and recommendations from relatives and friends. The current prediction shows how many cars will (most probably) be sold next month, but also highlights which factors the company could change to improve sales. This is important information to any business user.

Let's look at the statistical language R with SAP HANA, SAP Predictive Analytics and SAS Predictive Modeling Workbench for SAP HANA, which are optimized to run with or on SAP HANA. At the end of this chapter, we briefly look at the IBM SPSS modeler and MATLAB.

Analytics components in the SAP HANA context are mainly linked to the data digestion and storage layer because the functionalities and features of analytics applications are mostly pushed down and executed by SAP HANA directly.

2.5.1 SAP HANA and R

The language R was originally created as an open source project for statistical use and was initially more widespread in the scientific field. However, because it is an open source project, and everyone can contribute with new packages, its value was soon recognized across industries as a tool for predictive analytics. Packages in this context are a coded set of functions which, when installed on the server or client, can be called and executed.

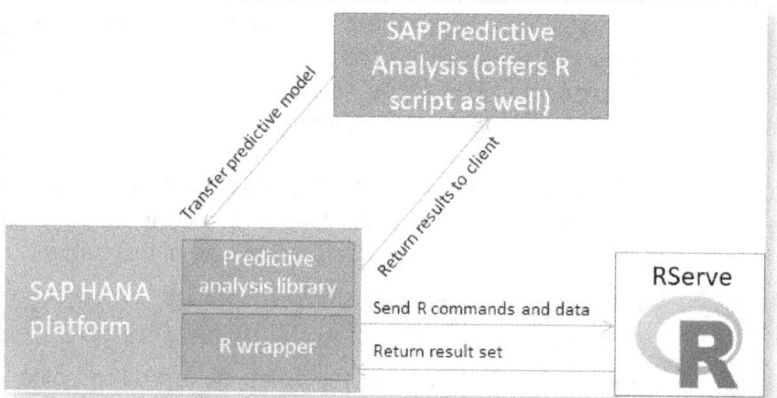

Figure 2.9: Simplified SAP predictive environment

Figure 2.9 shows a simplified representation of the interaction between the SAP predictive component, SAP HANA and R.

From an architectural perspective, in order to run R code, RServe needs to be installed on the SAP HANA Server (or a different, connected Server). It provides the option to execute any R code on the server side (R code is normally executed on the client side). Any R package required within the execution needs to be installed on RServe by the administrator. The installation of RServe is very simple in Linux and Windows, and requires administrator rights.

> **R integration guide**
>
>  A very detailed guide for installing and integrating R in combination with SAP HANA can be found on the SAP help pages:
>
> *https://help.sap.com/viewer/a78d7f701c3341339fafe4031b 64f015/2.0.01/en-US*

Once RServe is installed, R code can be executed from SAP HANA via an R wrapper component, or via a script created in the SAP Predictive Analytics tool and pushed down to SAP HANA. This means that you can program R code as a procedure, but you declare the procedure as RLang and not as SQL. For further information, please refer to the integration guide mentioned above.

In general, R is a very rich language and with the right package installed, you can cover most of the algorithms discovered in statistics and data mining. Additionally, the easy integration with SAP HANA makes it worth considering in any predictive scenario. However, there are some distinct disadvantages when using R with SAP HANA (when compared to other predictive analytics tools):

1. **Another coding language**—Although R as a language is relatively simple, it still requires you to learn the syntax for each algorithm before being able to write a function properly.

2. **The syntax check**—As R is not an integral part of SAP HANA studio, code checks are very difficult within SAP HANA itself. There is an R plugin for eclipse, but it does not really resolve the general problem. So, the only way to check code involves running it in your own RStudio.

3. **No direct execution in SAP HANA**—The R code is executed in RServe itself, which is not optimized for in-memory execution and,

55

therefore, will never be as fast as an execution within SAP HANA. In particular, processing large amounts of data might be problematic.

> **R use with SAP HANA**
>
>  In general, we recommend using the R integration only with SAP Predictive Analytics or other predictive analytics tools. They offer out-of-the-box functionality and only require programming in R for very specific functions. A direct use with SAP HANA only makes sense when you are already an expert in coding in R/SQL.

Note that it is also possible to execute R functions in the SAP Analytics Cloud when building stories. For that, the SAP Analytics Cloud needs to be set up with RServe enabled.

2.5.2 SAP Predictive Analytics

SAP Predictive Analytics has a long history of development but, so far, has not often been productively deployed by our customers. However, with each release of SAP Predictive Analytics, the number of supported algorithms has grown as steadily as the functionality of the tool itself.

As shown previously in Figure 2.9, SAP Predictive Analytics has a direct interaction with SAP HANA. This interaction makes it possible to export models directly to SAP HANA and to execute these models in the database itself, thereby leveraging the calculation power of SAP HANA. Any results generated by the model can then be viewed again via SAP Predictive Analytics, if required.

Furthermore, with the latest releases, this tool now belongs to the Business Objects suite and consists mainly of the following components:

- ▶ **Data Manager**—Some business users know little about predictions and statistics, and this tool helps them to prepare the data so it can be used for statistical algorithms. Columns are defined more specifically with their data type or their statistical type.

- **Automated Analytics**—The user can choose (supported by Automated Analytics) which statistical calculation to perform, without requiring any deeper knowledge of formulas or statistical models. Automated Analytics, together with the data manager, is the successor of what was called KXEN or Infinite Insights in earlier releases.
- **Expert analytics**—For more detailed analysis, Expert Analytics offers many algorithms which can be executed sequentially. This is especially relevant when building a larger model with more sophisticated analyses and a higher number of predictions. This tool is the successor of the original Predictive Analytics tool (version 1.X).
- **Predictive Factory**—The Predictive Factory allows for automated execution, retraining or revaluation of models created. This feature is very important when models are used productively.

Further information on SAP Predictive Analytics

More information on the modules of SAP Predictive Analytics can be found here:

https://help.sap.com/doc/e6fab47a74504646990b652a9f1d74e7/3.1/en-US/pa31_architecture_spec_en.pdf

The Expert Analytics tool also lets users integrate an R code into the predictive model and makes using it much simpler because the wrapper function itself is created without actually having to code it.

As the components show, most of the data mining, statistical and machine learning algorithms are delivered out-of-the-box and no deeper coding knowledge is needed. This is a clear differentiator for R. An exception is when you require specific algorithms which are not available in the SAP Predictive Analytics dictionary. When using SAP Predictive Analytics, especially Expert Analytics, statistical knowledge is required. Users should have insights into which algorithms perform best for the task, what the algorithm does, and which input parameters are required for the execution. Additionally, an understanding of how to statistically model data and variables is essential for SAP Predictive Analytics.

> **SAP Predictive Analytics**
>
>
> SAP has made significant investment in the area of predictive analytics, but has not yet closed the gap between it and the established providers. Therefore, we recommend SAP Predictive Analytics for simple predictive models only.

2.5.3 SAS Predictive Modeling Workbench for SAP HANA

SAS has a long-standing partnership with SAP; they offered an SAP BW integration with their models early on. Now, SAS has gone one step further and offers, in addition to their own in-memory-server (SAS LASR Analytic Server), an integration of their tool palette with the most common in-memory databases such as Teradata or SAP HANA. Additionally, SAS released a component called SAS Embedded Process, which aims to push down coding into databases or Big Data clusters, thereby leveraging already existing environments. With this approach, SAS appears to be the most innovative and integrative vendor in the market and helps customers to keep their technology stack lean. Other vendors, such as IBM, usually only offer this feature with their own databases.

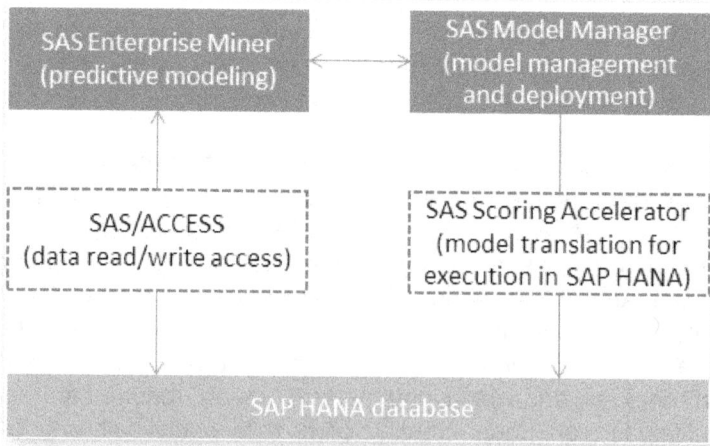

Figure 2.10: SAS predictive environment specific to SAP HANA

The SAS Predictive Modeling Workbench for SAP HANA continues this approach by delivering SAP HANA specific coding and tools out-of-the-box.

Figure 2.10 provides a simple overview of the tools which are part of the SAS Predictive Modeling Workbench, and their main interactions.

The following is a short explanation of what the different components offer:

- **SAS Enterprise Miner**—The SAS Enterprise Miner offers a graphical modeling environment with an extensive set of out-of-the-box algorithms for preparing and converting data, and creating predictive models. There is also an R integration.
- **SAS/ACCESS**—This component provides read and write access to HANA data, including the use of SAP HANA views.
- **SAS Model Manager**—Similar to the SAP predictive factory, the SAS Model Manager offers training, deployment and revaluation of models created.
- **SAS Scoring Accelerator**—When models are deployed to SAP HANA, the SAS Scoring Accelerator translates these models for execution in the SAP HANA database.

In addition to the predictive modeling workbench component for SAP HANA, there is also the SAS High-Performance Predictive Modeling Workbench for SAP HANA, which enables the development of models in-memory and does not require executing models on a separate server or on the client machine before the actual deployment. This is especially helpful in large data volume environments.

SAS offers one of the most sophisticated predictive modeling toolsets in the market. Historically, it was used mainly in banking and insurance. Due to its good integration with SAP HANA and Big Data environments, it is, in our opinion, the best choice when designing and implementing an SAP HANA-based predictive analytics solution.

> **Further material on SAS Predictive Modeling Workbench for SAP HANA**
>
>  For further information on the way SAS interacts with SAP HANA, we recommend reading the following white paper:
>
> http://support.sas.com/resources/papers/proceedings15/SAS1856-2015.pdf

2.5.4 Other predictive analytics tools

The tool with the largest market share in the predictive analytics area is SPSS Modeler. SPSS Modeler also offers a graphical modeling environment with a large number of out-of-the-box algorithms, as well as an R integration. One downside of the SPSS modeler (in our SAP HANA context) is the inability to push code down into SAP HANA. Instead, data needs to be loaded into a separate SPSS in-memory engine.

Another tool with a large market share is MATLAB. MATLAB is similar to R in that it relies on its own programming language; this also needs to be learned if you are new to it. MATLAB also brings its own database and code cannot be pushed into SAP HANA.

2.6 Front-end tools

A good BI architecture requires tools that enable the end user to consume data provided by the backend system (data consumption layer). These tools should not only fulfill the purpose of being able to consume data, but also need to satisfy requirements concerning user experience and analysis functions. The range of uses and demands towards front-end tools is diverse. Where some users might want to look at single data sets (e.g. one customer order), others might be interested in dashboards showing the whole picture (e.g. how many orders were placed in each month of the year and how much revenue was achieved). In this section, we present different front-end tools and take a closer look at their:

- usage scenarios,
- target audience,
- intended developer group, and
- integration with different sources.

We have decided to focus on a subset of the more well-known market leaders. We have taken into consideration the assessments of Gartner and Forester, as well as our own project experience, and the following products are in scope: SAP's BusinessObjects suite, SAP Fiori/SAPUI5, Tableau, QlikView/QlikSense, and the Microsoft BI reporting suite, specifically MS Power BI.

2.6.1 SAP BusinessObjects suite

SAP BusinessObjects started out as a separate company, designing alternative reporting solutions, and was acquired by SAP in 2007. BusinessObjects is now SAP's primary reporting suite. Query Designer (formerly known as BEx (Business Explorer) Query Designer) still plays a key role as an interface to SAP BW, and enables the design of queries which can be used by any frontend.

The SAP BusinessObjects suite consists of several tools, some of which have been discontinued over the years, and some of which are new additions, based on new SAP developments. The products which, as of today, will continue to be offered are as follows:

- **WebIntelligence (WebI)**—This is the only remaining product of the original BusinessObjects suite. WebI is very good at combining structured data from different sources and adding calculated measures or attributes via universes and reports; the results of which can be shown in tabular or chart format. Originally intended as a solution which could be developed by business users, it has become more of a tool for power users and IT developers. The target audience is middle and upper management. From a usability perspective, WebI fails to provide the modern look that other tools offer the end user.

- **Analysis for Microsoft Office**—Microsoft Excel users are typically in finance or controlling, and favor it due to the seemingly endless possibilities for manipulating data and performing calculations. This product offers report integration in Excel or PowerPoint, with backend data from SAP HANA or SAP BW. Tabular reports can be shown in Excel, and provide the possibility for simple drilldowns. Users are mostly specialists within a company. The report development depends on the design in the backend, because BEx queries or SAP HANA information views typically are used for this type of report.

- **Design Studio**—When it comes to web reporting and mobile reporting, Design Studio is currently the tool of choice in SAP'S reporting environment. Design studio is SAPUI5/HTML5-based and enables the creation of reports with HTML parameters, using standard charts and tables created within the SAPUI5 repertoire. The reports can be built on SAP Netweaver, SAP BW, SAP HANA, SAP Business Objects (BO) Universe, or a CSV file (comma separated values). The target audience is middle and upper management, but to develop these reports an IT specialist is required. If managed correctly, Design Studio delivers modern designs.

- **Lumira**—The newest self-service BI tool in SAP'S collection is Lumira. You can combine data from different sources, including Hadoop and other Big Data sources. This feature is especially useful when exploring new data sources and defining new KPIs or reports. It therefore appeals to data scientists and forward-thinking business users in particular. Because it is so user-friendly, business users can develop their own reports on the Lumira Web or Desktop.

> **SAP Lumira 2.0**
>
>  With SAP Lumira 2.0, Design Studio and SAP Lumira have been converged. From now on, the two products will be called SAP Lumira Designer (formerly Design Studio) and SAP Lumira Discovery (previously SAP Lumira). This change involves a combined server module for both the tools, but still two client applications. For further information, please see SAP's blog post, with Q&As:
>
> *https://help.sap.com/viewer/3dbb00422a214e39970963651f8a3094/ 2.2.0.0/en-US*

In conclusion, the SAP BusinessObjects Suite works very well with SAP's products. However, there are restrictions when connecting to sources from other vendors. When working with Big Data platforms, only SAP Lumira enables the user to connect directly; but this will mostly not be the tool of choice for report developers in IT. Apart from Lumira, only the SAP Business Objects Universe enables limited connectivity options to Oracle Essbase, SAS and Microsoft SQL Server Analysis Services or the other tools in the SAP BO Suite.

2.6.2 SAP Fiori and SAPUI5

The foundation of SAPUI5 was outlined as part of the XSA engine in Section 2.1.3. However, further considerations are necessary when considering SAPUI5 as a frontend; and it is worth mentioning the possibility to reuse tables and charts that can then be inserted into custom webpages. Their content can be defined by the developer. Because SAPUI5 is integrated in JavaScript and HTML code, it basically covers the scale of SAP Design Studio, but with much more design freedom. On the downside, developers have to code everything, whereas in Design Studio, the program code is automatically generated. If custom webpages and reports are required, SAPUI5 can be a great help in creating them.

SAP Fiori is also SAPUI5-based and offers apps especially for the Netweaver platform, including various LOBs of SAP S/4HANA. For SAP S/4HANA, it is the new state-of-the-art, front-end tool. The SAP Fiori Apps are considered enhancements (and in some cases replacements) of the traditional SAP Netweaver-based transactions, and deliver many additional features including operational reports. SAP Fiori can only be used with the SAP Netweaver platform and the target audience is restricted mostly to operational users. SAP Fiori is now available in Version 2.0, with an even better user experience.

> **Exploring SAPUI5 and Fiori**
>
> For a great demonstration of all the features available out-of-the-box in SAPUI5 (with the code attached), see: *https://sapui5.hana.ondemand.com/#/controls/*
>
> If you are interested in all the applications that have been created for SAP Fiori, a complete list can be found here: *https://fioriappslibrary.hana.ondemand.com/sap/fix/externalViewer/*

2.6.3 Tableau

Over the last few years, Tableau has gained more and more attention with business users due to its ease of use and very modern designs. Tableau acts as an independent vendor of visualization software and does not produce any other software (as of November 2016). This specialization makes the tool quite remarkable because it can connect to a large number of data sources, including Big Data sources such as Cloudera, Google BigQuery, and HortonWorks Hive.

Additionally, Tableau has a connectivity option to SAP BW (Versions 7.4 and higher) and SAP HANA. It can connect to InfoProviders and BEx queries, as well as import hierarchy information and other metadata. The connection is established via SAP OLE DB. For SAP HANA, the connection is an ODBC connection, and input parameters and variables are supported. SAP HANA hierarchies are not supported and need to be flattened out in order to use them in Tableau.

When it comes to data storage, Tableau does not require additional storage of data on the Tableau Server. Most users are of the opinion, however, that it makes sense to get an extract and store the data on the server. This enables faster drilldown in reports, compared to transferring data from SAP HANA during report execution.

Finally, reports can be designed and used by any business user; however, the intended target audience seems to be middle and higher management.

> **Connectivity information**
>
>
>
> For a full list of supported data sources and further detailed information on Tableau features, we recommend the well-documented online help at:
>
> *http://onlinehelp.tableau.com/current/pro/desktop/en-us/help.htm*

2.6.4 QlikView and Qlik Sense

The company Qlik is one of the leading BI Self-Service tool providers and one of the favorites among business users. Right from the beginning, QlikView was viewed critically by many IT departments because it required the loading of data onto a separate server and into cubes. This led to data duplication, which occurred often outside of the control / responsibility of IT. Today, querying directly on the source system is a good option, but is still not the preferred approach for QlikView.

QlikView is a dashboarding tool providing reports to business users in a well-formatted design. The data-loading mechanism needs to be developed by the IT department, but the report design can be done by power users.

The other tool produced by Qlik is Qlik Sense which represents a self-service BI tool enabling the end user to perform data discovery activities. Reports can be easily built and used by business users.

Both QlikView and Qlik Sense offer a set of connectors to load data from a large number of Big Data sources as well as SAP BW and SAP HANA.

> **Qlik connectors**
>
>  For an overview of supported connectors, we recommend the Qlik connector page:
>
> *https://help.qlik.com/en-US/connectors/Content/Home.htm*

2.6.5 Microsoft BI reporting suite

Microsoft offers a set of tools for working with data. Looking at the portfolio, you find Power BI (cloud-based analytical services), Power BI Desktop (stand-alone client application), Power BI Mobile (app for mobile devices), and Power BI Embedded (Azure-based service to add interactive Power BI reports into your own applications).

The core of these toolsets is a combination of the existing tools within Microsoft Excel, and consists of Microsoft Power Query, Power Pivot, Power View, and the recently added Power Map. The integration and evolvement of these Microsoft Excel plugins started with Microsoft Office 2010 and is now available with Microsoft Excel and Office 365 in professional editions. Let's take a brief look at the functionality offered by these plugins:

- **Power Query**—Microsoft has concentrated on providing a tool for loading and transforming data from different sources into Excel. With Power Query only the name has changed, but it offers the well-known "data" tab functionality which was slightly enhanced with Microsoft Excel 2016. Power Query includes connectivity to several sources such as SAP HANA and Teradata, but not SAP BW or any Big Data sources (as of 2016).

- **Power Pivot**—Power Pivot enables you to manipulate the data in the form of Pivot tables, including Data Analysis Expressions (DAX), which include Excel calculation functions such as SUM, DATE and many more.

- **Power View**—When users want to create a well-arranged report for printable documents, they can use the Power View plugin. The charts or tabular reports can be added to the page with further additions such as drop-down boxes.

▶ **Power Map**—This recent addition to the Excel Power suite plugins enables users to create 3D maps, based on table data that includes geographical information in several formats.

All these plugins can be easily developed and used by business users. They are also combined with the Microsoft Power BI desktop tool.

The Microsoft Power BI desktop adds further features to the MS Excel Power plugins; for example, the desktop client is much easier to handle and publishes dashboards and reports in HTML5 format. In that regard, it is similar to SAP Design Studio/SAP Lumira Designer (with SAP Lumira 2.0). It is also possible to work with Power BI on a Web interface.

The **Power BI** suite is able to connect to both SAP BW and SAP HANA, as well as to some Big Data connectors, including Apache Spark, Apache Impala, and to the Hadoop file system directly. As the SAP BW has been added recently, some features such as dependent InfoObjects are not supported. The connector does not support live data loads and data needs to be loaded to the Power BI application first. In comparison, SAP HANA client offers direct query which works on live data.

Finally, Power BI integrates well with Microsoft SharePoint and the Microsoft Azure cloud.

> **Microsoft Power BI**
>
>  For further information on Microsoft Power BI and supported connectors, we recommend visiting the documentation page which lists all the connectors:
>
> *https://powerbi.microsoft.com/en-us/documentation/powerbi-desktop-use-directquery/*

For the sake of completeness, we will now mention SQL Server Reporting Services (SSRS), which has long been available. This tool enables users to create reports formatted for use in document form. Mobile apps have also been supported since SSRS 2012. SSRS offers several connections, including SAP BW and Teradata. However, we believe that working with Microsoft Power BI is the best way forward for dashboard design in the Microsoft tool suite.

2.6.6 Tabular comparison

Table 2.2 summarizes the different frontends discussed in this section. We have not looked at functionality because in building a BI architecture, the options and features of integrating the front-end tool into the environment are more crucial than the functionality of the tool itself.

Tool/ Criteria	SAP BO suite	SAPUI5/ SAP Fiori	Tableau	QlikView / QlikSense	Microsoft Power BI
Target audience	Operational level to upper management	Operational level	Middle to upper management	Middle to upper management	Middle to upper management
Usage scenarios	Excel reporting to dashboarding, data exploration	Operational reporting and transactions	Data exploration, dashboarding	Data exploration, dashboarding	Data exploration, dashboarding
Developer type (0 - ++)[1]	Depending on the tool—0 (e.g. SAP Design studio) to ++ (e.g. Analysis for office)	0	++	0 (QlikView), ++ (QlikSense)	++
SAP Connectivity (0 - ++)[2]	++	++	+	+	+
Connectivity to Big Data platforms (0 - ++)[3]	0—with the exception of SAP Lumira, there is none	0	++	++	+
Connectivity to other sources (0 - ++)[3]	+ (via Universe or SAP Lumira)	0	++	++	++

Table 2.2: Comparison of SAP BO, SAPUI5/Fiori, Tableau and Qlik

---

[1] Developer type is defined as "0" (business user with little knowledge of technology), to "++" (an IT developer).

[2] SAP Connectivity is defined as "0" (little or no connectivity), to "++" (all features of the SAP data source are supported).

[3] Connectivity is defined as "0" (no sources are supported), to "++" (many sources are supported—at least 5 or 6).

2.7 Big Data ecosystems

Big Data—you can no longer ignore it when designing a holistic enterprise information system (or do you still see Big Data as the new kid on the block?). We recognize that dealing with huge amounts of data has, for years, been a challenge. Massive hardware investments have been made, and new architectural concepts have been developed, in order to work with/on data. In the context of business intelligence, the data warehousing concept and separation of OLTP and OLAP processing are a prominent example of this approach. So, is the term "Big Data" not just the next evolution step in the area of handling massive amounts of data in today's world? But what exactly is it? When do we talk about Big Data, and when do we need to apply associated technologies? In our reference architecture, we see this technology stack as an integral part of a modern data digestion and storage layer also having direct interfaces to upstream and downstream systems.

Big Data is generally characterized by the three "V"s—**Volume**, **Variety**, and **Velocity**:

- ▶ **Volume** refers to the massive amount of poly-structured data coming, for example, from transaction logs, machine sensors, and click-streams. We are talking about data volumes of petabytes in contrast to classic data warehouse solutions handling sizes of several terabytes.

- ▶ **Variety** refers to the vast spectrum of data types and its origins handled in a Big Data environment.

- ▶ **Velocity** refers to the high speed for creating or updating data, as well as the short time needed to analyze the data.

In some definitions, the aspects of data **Value** and **Validity** (e.g. for a specific research area) are also considered. For the scope of this book, we understand Big Data as a combination of technologies and known methods to build highly scalable environments for handling and processing massive amounts of versatile data. From our perspective, Big Data starts where traditional ways of storing and analyzing data end. Therefore, Big Data complements the endeavors defined under the umbrella of Business Intelligence.

In contrast to the idealistic claims of harmonized, quality-assured, and integrated data in data warehouses, Big Data aims to access and analyze the data as soon as it is created. Thus, its origin, and the benefit of low-cost and flexible data provisioning, actually lies in bypassing or ignoring ETL concepts. The as-yet unfulfilled integration and harmonization intensions of data warehouse solutions also apply to Big Data solutions.

In the vast field of Big Data-related concepts and technologies, the **data lake** approach has taken its place over the last few years. The main idea is to store data in its native format, regardless of whether it consists of a raw, structured, semi-structured, or completely unstructured definition. A data lake provides a structure for holding a vast amount of data at a low cost while simultaneously providing the opportunity to discover connections and insights within it. Therefore, a data element is marked with identifier and metadata tags, which help to find the relevant data for a specific (preselected) query and downstream analysis. Data lake users are typically analysts and data scientists.

Storing all possible relevant data, for any purpose which might arise in the future, sounds like the ultimate dream come true, and not only for data-driven companies. But, to leverage the tremendous potential and opportunity, a sound governance framework needs to be in place, taking into consideration aspects such as central definition of semantics and KPIs, data origin and ownership, reliability, and validity period. Context and metadata for each data point in your data lake are key for precise tagging and data usage.

As the data lake concept is maturing, more and more companies are trying to implement this highly agile approach as their single store of data. Common entry points and technological foundations are cloud storage services such as Amazon S3, Azure Blob storage, and even more well-known, the distributed file system of Apache Hadoop.

Everyone working in the Big Data world knows about Apache Hadoop, the pioneering framework which was developed years ago, inspired by Google File System and the MapReduce algorithm. Today, this open-source software framework provides a combination of algorithms and file system concepts, enabling highly scalable, distributed computing across clustered servers. Each server adds a piece of local calculation and storage capacity. Within this environment, a query on any large set of data is spread and processed across the clusters. Programming modules ensure service availability and reliability at application level.

At its core, Apache Hadoop consists of the following modules:

- **HDFS** (Hadoop Distributed File System) is the distributed file system and is able to store enormous volumes of data in inexpensive commodity hardware.
- The **YARN** (Yet Another Resource Negotiator) framework for resource and cluster management reconciles how applications use Hadoop system resources.
- The **MapReduce** component enables massive parallel processing on large data sets across compute clusters.
- **Common Utilities** provides administration and support for the other modules.

Apache Hadoop projects

 Open-source software is rapidly evolving, and you can check the latest updates on Hadoop projects at *http://hadoop.apache.org/*. You can also visit the corresponding wiki pages maintained by the Apache Software Foundation, which deal with many questions regarding individual projects and technologies: *https://cwiki.apache.org*.

Under the Apache Hadoop umbrella, several related projects and sub-projects have been founded, and are a firm component in Big Data ecosystems today. These include:

- **HBase** is an open-source, distributed, NoSQL (not only SQL) database running on top of Hadoop and HDFS. It provides real-time data access capabilities on very large tables (in the range of billions of rows and several million columns) with low latency and low tendency to errors. The **Cassandra** database is comparable. Both use many key concepts of Google's Bigtable definition as their foundation.
- **Hive** also builds on the Hadoop foundation and consists of a data warehouse infrastructure. Following classic data warehousing ideas, Hive is designed for data aggregation, ad hoc querying,

71

and analysis. It uses SQL for reading and writing large sets of data in distributed storage. A Java Database Connectivity (JDBC) driver is available to connect to Hive from 3rd party tools.

- **Spark** is a general engine for very fast processing of large-scale data, enabling applications to run several times faster in-memory than with Hadoop MapReduce. Spark can be leveraged for various types of applications such as stream processing, machine learning, graph computation, and ETL-like data transformations. Spark can access multiple data sources such as HDFS, HBase, Cassandra, and Amazon S3. Programming of applications can be done in Java, Scala, Python, or R. Scala should be the preferred option because it is Spark's origin language.

- **Storm** has as a main aim to deliver distributed, real-time computation of large volumes of data characterized by high velocity. The features of Storm are the handling of unbounded streams of data, and the real-time processing of complex events, in a fault-tolerant manner (in contrast to Hadoop's offering for batch processing). Storm is commonly combined with **Kafka**, a distributed streaming platform optimized for high throughput. Kafka contains a robust queue for high volumes of data, allowing point-to-point transfer of messages, which are maintained in categories called topics. In a Big Data scenario, Kafka can be positioned as preprocessor for Storm (e.g. streaming data is sent to Kafka and Storm pulls the data from there).

- **Sqoop** provides efficient transfer of bulk data between structured sources (e.g. relational databases) and Hadoop. It enables bi-directional communications such as importing data into HDFS, populating tables in HBase or Hive Metastore (referring to the table present in HDFS), and exporting data to a relational database. Sqoop uses MapReduce jobs internally to do the data processing work.

With regard to the design of holistic BI Architectures, we have chosen to outline only a subset of modules and projects in the constantly growing Hadoop area. In addition, we have decided not to discuss the main distributions of Cloudera (*http://www.cloudera.com/*), MapR (*https://www.mapr.com/*), and Hortonworks (*http://hortonworks.com/*), and we only mention their online presence here. Please note, Cloudera and Hortonworks have recently announced to merge into one company (*http://vision.cloudera.com/cloudera-hortonworks-from-the-edge-to-ai*).

Now that we have learned about the key technological elements in the Big Data space, we would like to highlight that there are also reference architectures in Big Data. As always, there is not only the one truth. For the purposes of this book, we outline below common terms and the most common definitions of each, which we have adopted:

- **Data ingestion** describes the process of obtaining and importing data into designated storage locations; for example, by using Sqoop, Kafka or other adapter technologies.

- **Data storage/staging** is the layer designed for holding (tagged) data of any kind for further processing (e.g. HDFS, HBase).

- **Data processing** involves all operations for distilling and working on the data for any desired purpose (e. g. HIVE, Storm, Spark).

- **Data consumption** covers services for visualizing, exploring, and analyzing, or for any other data-driven approach to gaining new insights from your data. A wide range of tools fit into this area such as R, R-Shiny, D3.js, SAS®, SAP Business Objects, or Tableau.

- **Operation and Scheduling** is a cross-functional layer responsible for effectively managing the available resources within a cluster. YARN, ZooKeeper, Ambari, and Oozie are popular examples in this field.

Big Data architecture

A good starting point for designing Big Data architectures is the LAMBDA architecture approach. An introduction, and examples, can be found at: *http://lambda-architecture.net/*. Depending on your use case, the Kappa approach might be also of interest: *www.kappa-architecture.com/*.

It took a while for enterprises to accept and adopt the emerging open-source Big Data technologies for their own businesses. To be honest, for a long time, the level of maturity of Big Data modules also prevented its extensive use in professional environments. Today, many enterprises successfully run huge cluster farms and benefit from the tremendous potential (still only partially discovered), which is slumbering in their data. Therefore, it is not only a question of finding valuable synopses in known segments or optimizing existing processes, but rather of spotting, scouting and entering into completely new business areas.

Coming back to our initial assessment, in claiming that Big Data is an evolutionary step in Business Intelligence, we see it as a clear move away from predefined, structured reporting of known artefacts towards insight-driven analytics. From our perspective, Big Data has proven its enterprise-readiness in various projects and the added value is obvious. On that note, we rate and recommend Big Data as an excellent complement to traditional data warehouse concepts.

Big Data and SAP HANA

We already know about the capabilities and power of SAP HANA. Now imagine combining this with Hadoop's strength in storing and processing large amounts of data in a cost-effective way. The result would have to be a new dimension of rich and insight-driven analytics. Before diving into the technological options to connect these two worlds, let's determine some general usage scenarios:

- **Smart, scalable data storage**—Storing data in SAP HANA's memory is expensive, whereas one of Hadoop's core competencies is to store large data types and huge data quantities cost-effectively. Besides other parameters such as type and ownership of data, a self-evident approach is to keep often-used data in-memory at the SAP HANA side and move data that is only occasionally needed to Hadoop. Thus, leveraging Hadoop in a hot-warm-cold scenario is a cheap and scalable storage for cold data.

- **Hadoop analytics for SAP HANA**—When it comes to data processing, Hadoop's focus is on analytics on its vast spectrum of available data. The idea behind this is to compute the analytics algorithms on the Hadoop side and enrich the SAP HANA reporting by sending only the Hadoop results to SAP HANA. Of course, the reverse is also possible, by pushing SAP HANA analytics results into the Hadoop cluster.

- **Joint Reporting**—This is possibly the most challenging approach in this list. The basic concept sounds simple because, in one single SAP HANA report, data stored in the Hadoop cluster is combined with data coming directly from SAP HANA via joint characteristics. In addition to the recurring questions regarding data quality, leading master data, etc., at the technical level, the main challenge is the speed of data processing, which differs significantly between the two. Therefore, often an asynchronous approach might be the most feasible.

But how can SAP HANA and Hadoop now interact with each other? A list of selected technological approaches is given below:

- **Smart Data Access (SDA)** offers one-way communication, accessing structured data on the Hadoop cluster triggered from SAP HANA in real-time. Upon request, SDA pulls data from the remote source and provides it via virtual tables to any data consumer. By default, the remote data is not stored in SAP HANA. The setup of SDA requires the creation of a remote connection to Hive using Open Database Connectivity (ODBC). The appropriate ODBC driver (e.g. Simba ODBC Driver) must be installed on the SAP HANA server and registered in the .odbc.ini file. By using MapReduce or Spark (which offers higher performance), data from Hive tables or Spark Resilient Distributed Datasets (RDD) can be retrieved.

- **SAP HANA Spark Controller** enables access to Hadoop through a Spark SQL interface to Hive. On the SAP HANA side, you simply create a remote data source analogue following the procedure described with SDA. Therefore, a migration of existing SDA scenarios based on ODBC is very possible. The Spark SQL Adapter is the only plug-in needed to enable an exchange between the SDA framework and the Spark Controller, which again is deployed on the Hadoop side. YARN and Spark Assembly JAR are used to connect SAP HANA with HDFS (through Hive and Spark). SAP recommends using the Spark controller over SDA because it provides better performance and additional integration with SAP Vora. As of SPS 12, there is also a connection to the Data Lifecycle Manager (DLM).

- **SAP Data Services** is the mature and rich data-transfer product within SAP's portfolio, providing full ETL functionality. For several years now there has been a close integration with SAP HANA. On the Hadoop side, it is possible to interact with Hive and handle HDFS files (e.g. via Pig scripts). The benefit of the predominantly in-batch processing within SAP Data Services is its transformation engine which enables the conversion of unstructured data from Hadoop before sending it to SAP HANA. The communication between SAP HANA and Hadoop via SAP Data Services is bidirectional.

- **Sqoop** is another tool for bidirectional, batch-oriented transfer of bulk data between Hadoop and SAP HANA. As Sqoop originates from the Apache project, it is maintained from the Hadoop side. A prerequisite is the installation of the SAP HANA JDBC drivers on the respective Hadoop directory.

- **SAP Vora** is probably the best-known way of creating connectivity and interaction between SAP HANA and Hadoop. However, there were many start-up difficulties and recent versions have come with many improvements and better support for current Spark versions. SAP Vora provides in-memory processing engines which run on the Hadoop side as an extension of the Spark framework. It is able to scale up to numerous nodes, thereby dealing with massive data in a distributed environment. SAP Vora can be accessed from SAP HANA by using either the SAP HANA Spark controller or, since SAP Vora 1.3, the proprietary SAP HANA Vora Remote Source Adapter (`voraodbc`). Analogue to SDA, the `voraodbc` remote connection, is required in order to create a virtual SAP HANA table for each object on the SAP Vora remote side. `SELECT`, `INSERT`, `UPDATE` statements are SQL commands which are supported when querying SAP Vora objects.

> **SAP HANA Hadoop integration—additional information**
>
>  Detailed and up-to-date information about the HANA Hadoop integration technologies can be found on SAP's help pages at:
>
> http://help.sap.com/saphelp_hanaplatform/helpdata/en/fd/ 3b8d1cbc074b889c8e06b05ba7af54/content.htm
>
> Specifics about SAP Vora are available at:
> http://help.sap.com/saphelp_hanaplatform/helpdata/en/7f/ 86c9cde0794c67b093932668b3d33c/content.htm.

From our perspective, all of these approaches were developed for good reason. Depending on the use, predominant knowledge, and leading technology, the best connector has to be determined. Linking the two worlds of SAP HANA and Big Data cannot be neglected in modern BI architectures, so it is essential to familiarize yourself with these components. We will return to this topic later in this book and deepen the foundations built in this chapter.

2.8 Cloud platforms

This section brings us to one of the most promoted and exciting technologies in recent years—cloud computing. In this section, we discuss this concept from an SAP HANA point of view. First, let us start with some fundamentals of cloud computing and the ways in which it can be used.

Looking at our reference architecture, it is not possible to clearly determine which layers are and which are not affected by the Cloud movement. Today, any layer (data generation, data digestion and storage, data consumption) can be fully realized in the cloud, and combined with on-premise solutions. We will learn more about this in the course of this chapter.

So, what is the cloud? How can I participate in the cloud movement? And what does it cost? What are the benefits for my business? Since the early introduction of computer systems into the professional business world, IT departments have invested significant time and effort in providing appropriate facilities for running expensive and sensitive hardware. The demand for powerful computing resources to be available around-the-clock, and with worldwide accessibility, is constantly increasing. This is evident in the number of large companies that are continuously expanding their IT infrastructures and building data centers. Data centers currently consist of on-premise server clusters with numerous high-performing nodes, and with multiple CPUs and huge memory capacities. For years, this has been the standard paradigm; having your own data center gives the advantage of full control over the individual hardware, middleware, and software installed on it. The data center approach is said to be highly customizable and scalable according to individual needs. An on-premise implementation is currently still the best-known delivery model for SAP customers. It allows as many modifications as required (e.g. in S/4HANA). The downside of modifications is the increased effort and costs involved when upgrading your solution to the next release, and when considering all implemented changes.

Calling a data center your own also forces you to take on control and responsibility for failure safety. This means that the infrastructure needs to fulfil parameters such as high-availability (i.e. redundancy of components) and backup mechanisms, as well as handle security at various levels. Running this complex IT infrastructure, and always keeping pace with technological innovations in order to meet future business needs is definitely not every company's key competence. Now, imagine if all concerns and woes associated with operating your own data center could be mitigated simply by subscribing to services offering high-performance computing and almost endless storage space? This is exactly where **cloud computing** comes into play.

Cloud computing refers to a shared pool of off-premise computing resources which is omnipresent, highly-available, accessible on demand via an internet connection, and controlled by a service provider. Service providers are specialized in offering high-performance computing resources and taking care of infrastructure maintenance and updates. They professionally operate extremely large data centers and offer their customers cost-effective use of these resources. In turn, customers benefit from easy, self-service access to resources, options to scale up or down their solution, and a kind of jump-start which does not require much time and capital. Cloud services offer across-the-board, tailored subscription plans; for instance, you can decide on a pay-per-use model (fitting to your budget restrictions) for exactly the computing power you need at specific times.

However, in a cloud-based environment, there are many entry and exit points which need to be secured. When cloud computing first began, many companies questioned the level of security of their data in the cloud. Cloud service providers worked hard to secure their environments against internal and external attacks. In addition, data protection rules differ across different geographic regions, and data centers had to be implemented with adherence to local data security guidelines. Therefore, specific customer needs and regulatory needs can be fulfilled.

Let's now distinguish between public, private, and hybrid cloud offerings:

- **Public cloud** can be defined as high-performing computing resources in an external data center, which you access via the internet (i.e. a public network). A service provider is responsible for infrastructure, hardware and software, in accordance with your selected requirements. Microsoft Azure and Amazon Web Services (AWS) offer some of the better-known public cloud offerings, including various alternatives (i.e. computing, storage, database, and network). Both provide options to run SAP solutions in their environments. SAP, as a service provider, has delivery models such as SAP Cloud Platform (SCP) and (partner) solutions, such as SuccessFactors, Concur, Ariba, or Fieldglass. Some S/4HANA offerings are also available as public cloud offerings, but are rarely chosen by customers. In its public cloud scenarios, SAP fully manages the software which means that updates are pushed according to an SAP-defined schedule. Configurations and extensions are tightly controlled.

- The main differentiator of a **private cloud** is that a service provider's infrastructure (or a specific part) runs exclusively for a single customer, or is run by the customer's own IT department. Even though the technical foundation is the same, access is highly secured either by an intranet environment or by a virtual private network (VPN) connection. The service provider, or the responsible IT department, manages the overall infrastructure. In comparison to the public cloud, it gives customers a higher level of freedom to customize and control their designated resources and services. With regard to security standards, your private cloud basically follows the standards of your service provider.

However, depending on your deployment scenario, a private cloud can also be set up within your own firewall. In the case of private clouds, payment is often made upfront and is considered a capital expense. Amazon Virtual Private Cloud (VPC) is a well-known service provider in this area. Microsoft has also entered the market with its private cloud platform option as part of the Azure stack. When looking at SAP, almost all of its cloud customers opt for a private cloud solution. The software is still managed by SAP, but updates are coordinated with the customer and software modifications are possible (with increased service fee, depending on the modification). The HANA Enterprise Cloud is yet another provider of this delivery model. S/4HANA offers also a private cloud option.

▶ **Hybrid cloud** is the combination of different delivery models. Up to now, this concept has not been widely used because it faces fundamental challenges in the overall environment design. For example, cloud resources could be used in calculation scenarios when the on-premise hardware reaches it limit. From an end-user perspective, this switch to the cloud should be seamless. Therefore, all infrastructure components need to be aligned in terms of application provisioning and security, in order to run and appear as one homogenous solution.

In addition to choosing between public or private cloud, there is also a choice between various business models in the long list of "as-a-service" solutions. We will now focus on the different layers of cloud computing, which are illustrated in Figure 2.8 and explained in the following section.

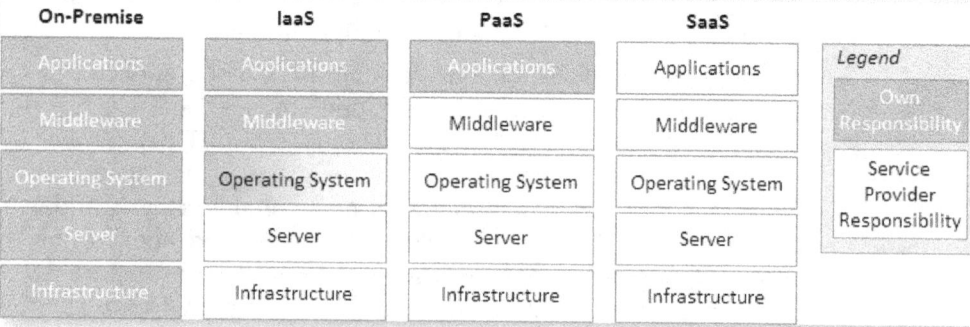

Figure 2.11: Layers of cloud computing

The schematic representation of the on-premise scenario is provided for comparison purposes. It highlights that maintaining a data center on-premise gives you full control, but also means taking responsibility for the actual applications, the middleware components, the installation and running of the operating systems, the server, and the infrastructure. Let's now look at the other business models of cloud support, and distinguish the different services provided by each one

- **Infrastructure as a service** (IaaS) provides off-premise hardware to ensure high-availability of computing resources for setting up your own application scenario, starting at the level of the operating system or above (depending on the defined IaaS portfolio). In addition, fast network connectivity, uninterrupted power supply, high-performing servers, and data storage as a computing backbone are provided and maintained by the service provider. IaaS solutions give direct access to either physical or virtual servers. In either case, your subscription can easily be scaled according to your needs. Pay-per-use is a typical commercial model in this scenario. As part of AWS, Amazon's Elastic Compute Cloud (EC2) is probably the best-known provider in this area. Microsoft Azure's Virtual Machines (VM) are also classified as IaaS. SAP's offering is **SAP HANA Enterprise Cloud** (HEC), which is a managed cloud service running in SAP's own data centers. It gives customers the freedom and flexibility to lift and shift existing applications (e.g. SAP BW, SAP Business Objects) or to deploy new solutions (e.g. SAP S/4HANA, custom developed programs) to the (private) cloud.

- **Platform as a Service** (PaaS) enhances typical infrastructure services by providing environments for the lifecycle of (cloud) application development and delivery (e.g. database and web services, runtime environments). Development is done via web-based access and subscription to the required tools and services. Both portfolios of AWS and Microsoft Azure contain PaaS services, as do the SAP HANA offerings. The corresponding offering from SAP in this context is the **SAP Cloud Platform** (SCP). SCP offers comprehensive services based on SAP HANA-enabling enhancements, customizations, and new application development (e.g. integration services, mobile services, business services, IoT services). A typical use for today's projects is the development of Fiori apps connecting to source systems, regardless of whether they are provided as SaaS, or as (custom) SAP or non-SAP applications hosted on-premise or in the HEC.

▶ **Software as a Service** (SaaS) covers everything needed to use specific software. The delivery model ranges from hosting to licensing all cost factors end-to-end, meeting pre-defined service level agreements. Installation and maintenance costs are therefore things of the past. There are countless products available as SaaS (e.g. Microsoft Office 365, eBay, SuccessFactors, Ariba). Running CRM software in the cloud is particularly popular. Cloud services from Amazon and Microsoft can be used for SaaS scenarios. As well as its cloud-based partner solutions, SAP offers **SAP Analytics Cloud,** its own SaaS-product which comes with SCP and therefore runs on SAP HANA. SAP Analytics Cloud provides services for real-time data discovery and visualization which meet planning and predictive demands.

SAP in the Cloud—overview of offerings

For the latest updates and information on the various SAP offerings in the cloud space, we recommend the following web page:
http://www.sap.com/solution/cloud.html

SAP solutions can also benefit from deployments and analytics services in Amazon Web Services, Microsoft Azure, or Google Cloud Platform. For a short introduction into this topic we recommend to read the following article: *http://buquati.com/blogs/sap-cloud-platform-neo-vs-cloud-foundry-cf/*.

In summing up all the technological options and flavors, what are the benefits of cloud computing? It is clear that moving to a cloud option gives you a transparent view of your IT-related costs and reduces risk with regard to capital expenses. Companies can focus all their energy and effort into expanding their key competencies. In this way, we also see benefits in being able to flexibly scale subscriptions for future needs. Furthermore, cloud solutions, especially at the PaaS and SaaS level, enable faster application development on the latest technologies, and thus drive business agility (and in the best case help to enter new markets or business models).

> **Total cost of ownership (TCO)—calculator for cloud solutions**
>
>  At a rudimentary level, there are TCO and benefits calculators which can give you an idea of the added value a move to the cloud can bring to your specific scenario. We suggest using these calculators only as an initial estimation and idea generator. Amazon's TCO calculator can be found at: *https://awstcocalculator.com/*.

However, with each level of additional service scope, you give up a certain amount of control over your ability to adjust the environment exactly to your needs. This does not mean that customization is not possible, but rather that it is limited, and may also incur additional charges. Whether a cloud offering is suitable for your specific scenario also depends on your performance requirements, security, and drive for innovation. We would like to emphasize that a cloud solution does not automatically mean a reduction in the complexity of your IT landscape. On the contrary, we see significantly greater complexity, especially during transition or in hybrid scenarios. Unquestionably, cloud computing is, or at least will become, a commodity. It is just a question of time and the available service portfolio that will determine when you join the movement.

2.9 Summary

In this chapter, we discussed the components of an SAP HANA BI architecture following the categorical layers of our reference architecture. We presented you with the technological foundation for each of these components and explained their importance for an innovative architecture.

In the first section, we looked at the core functionalities of the SAP HANA platform, including out-of-the-box features and add-ons.

Next, we covered SAP S/4HANA and Embedded Analytics.

We then presented the use of SAP BW/4HANA, its design and how it affects the whole BI architecture.

The concepts of loading and processing data within a BI landscape were part of the next section, where we outlined the differences between ETL and streaming technology. ETL tools such as Data Services, Smart Data Integration (SDI), and Sqoop were then briefly introduced. The second part of this section focused on different streaming tools' functions and used Kafka and Smart Data Streaming (SDS) as examples.

In the subsequent section, we elaborated on predictive analytics and discussed its use in business situations. We looked at available predictive analytics tools and focused on those that integrate best with SAP HANA.

The section on front-end tools reviewed the various tools available for our architecture scenarios. We focused on the SAP-based tool options, but also looked at and compared the other market leaders.

In the next section on Big Data ecosystems, we explained the (Big Data) tools that can be used well with SAP HANA. To begin with, we established a common understanding of the general concept and objective of Big Data and the data lake concept. Key modules of the Apache Hadoop project were introduced. In order to understand and build useful interfaces between SAP HANA and Hadoop, we drew a high-level layer concept for typical Big Data setups. We then discussed cooperation scenarios between SAP HANA and Hadoop.

Finally, we covered cloud platforms. We outlined the framework of data centers versus cloud computing, and differentiated public, private, and hybrid cloud objectives. This led us to the most common layers of cloud computing (IaaS, PaaS, SaaS). We then focused on the SAP cloud platforms SAP Cloud Platform (SCP), SAP HANA Enterprise Cloud (HEC), and the SAP Analytics Cloud.

3 SAP HANA BI architectures

In this chapter, we explore architectural scenarios, using the building blocks of an SAP HANA BI architecture. Our reference architecture will serve as a guideline. We finish the chapter with best practices in combining selected architectural options and we give recommendations on transformation roadmaps.

3.1 SAP HANA BI reference architecture

In this section, we progressively develop our SAP HANA BI reference architecture. Let's start with a general breakdown and overview of the data processing layers and the disciplines of working on, and with, the data. Figure 3.1 outlines the possible technologies involved and the corresponding architecture layers.

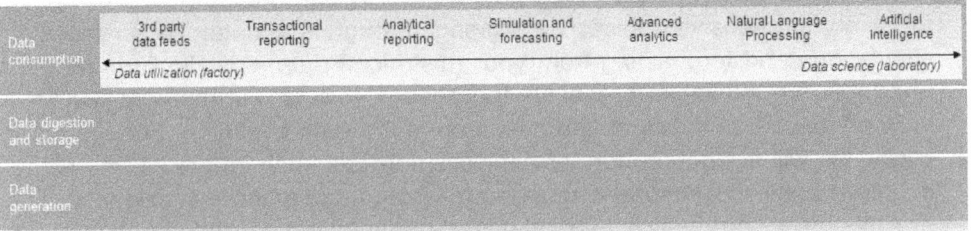

Figure 3.1: Reference layers—BI data processing

The bottom layer, **data generation,** represents the components that are able to create any kind of new data. Examples of such data include: a traditional ERP or CRM system, a billing system, an office application, a business-critical legacy system, a weather channel, a meter, a web crawler, a social media feed, a machine's sensor, and so on. Downstream systems deriving data from source systems are not classified as a member of the data generation layer. Regardless of the origin, format and technology used to generate the data, it needs to be processed for its respective usage.

85

The **data digestion and storage** layer refines and prepares the data from the layer below for further utilization. This can be a simple type conversion, a semantic tagging of the raw data, a consolidation or harmonization rule, or an operation to combine data coming from various sources. The scope and scale of solutions varies greatly; for example, it could include an entire data warehouse suite, a comprehensive ETL tool, a simple web service, a replication mechanism, or a messaging service.

As of today, there is a large variety of tools for consuming data. In the topmost layer, the **data consumption** layer, these tools are leveraged to provide the desired data, fine-tuned to the end-user needs. Examples of this could be: a simple projection or list of selected data, a tabular reporting based on transactional data, or an interactive user interface to work self-reliantly with the data. In the image above, the x-axis shows a wide range of data uses—from pure utilization of data to scientific work. Looking from left to right, the core data uses start with straightforward data feeds, to downstream tools and applications, and require no further logic. Next, is transactional reporting, leveraging data from source systems enriched with master data or minor calculations. This is followed by analytical reporting, which combines data from various sources and allows for a comprehensive toolset for digging through the data. To enable simulations and forecasting from your (historical) data, specific libraries and tools are available to achieve the desired results. Furthermore, we view advanced analytics as the next step in the data evolution. For simplicity, we will not go into further analytics subjects such as predictive or cognitive analytics. Natural language processing and artificial intelligence are the disciplines which use scientific methods the most to work on prepared data. The x-axis also shows a decrease in the maturity of tools, from left to right. We therefore consider tools and applications at the left end of this range to be easily manageable with established structures and methods (factory approach). At the right end, the complete opposite applies and these technologies apply to the fields of open research (laboratory approach).

Taking this layer concept as a basis, we now outline the technologies to design the reference architecture. Figure 3.2 illustrates the layers introduced previously and highlights key technologies for a comprehensive SAP HANA BI architecture, including the Big Data space. For each key technology, we have also added analytical elements and/or relevant data warehousing layers.

SAP HANA BI ARCHITECTURES

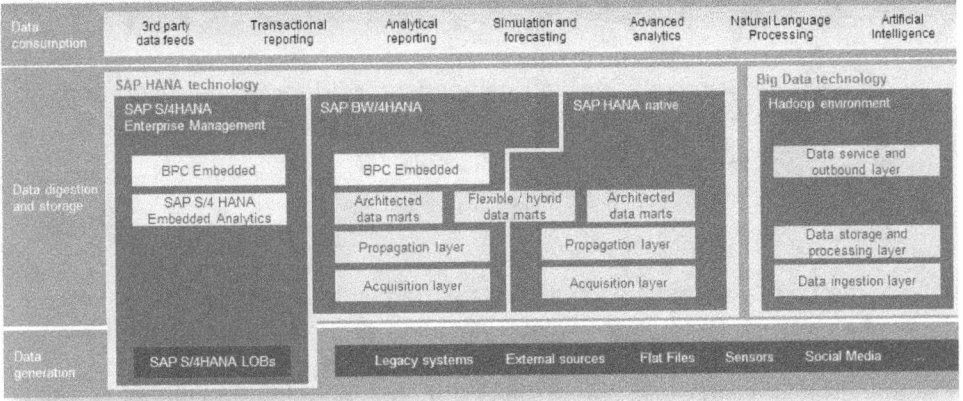

Figure 3.2: Reference layers—SAP BI and Big Data technologies

Let's start with the various LOBs of **SAP S/4HANA** on the data generation layer. Examples of other data generating systems were mentioned earlier and will not be discussed further here. With the SAP S/4HANA Embedded Analytics component, SAP S/4HANA not only generates transactional data within the LOBs, but also provides solutions for running reports and predefined analytics within its own environment (data digestion and storage layer). BPC embedded serves as SAP's main approach, completing the picture with planning, consolidating, and forecasting features for SAP S/4HANA. All relevant SAP S/4HANA elements for our reference architecture are included within the previously mentioned SAP S/4HANA Enterprise Management.

SAP BW/4HANA and **SAP HANA native** are similar, with regard to their architectural layers. Both are explicitly classified as data digestion and storage approaches and include the layers acquisition, propagation, and architected data marts. Virtualization of data should be taken into account, especially for the propagation and data mart layer. This essentially also follows SAP's LSA++ guideline (see Section 2.3). In addition to the architected data mart layer, we find strong arguments for a flexible, hybrid data mart layer spanning the highly-integrated SAP BW/4HANA world and the architectural openness in the SAP HANA native space. BPC embedded is also mentioned for planning, consolidation, and forecasting on the SAP BW/4HANA side. As a side note, the question of where to apply which kind of planning and consolidation solution, and for what purposes, in a BI architecture, is a subject for separate research and is therefore not covered here.

87

> **Data virtualization versus data persistency**
>
>  A discussion and comparison of data virtualization and data persistency can be found in our previous book: *SAP HANA Advanced Modeling*.

For the **Big Data** technology stack (see right side of Figure 3.2) we refer to the previously-introduced data ingestion and data storage and processing layers (see Section 2.7) as well as the data service and outbound layer. Within this, we position the components of a Hadoop environment.

Looking at the data consumption layer, on the left side we see standardized data provisioning cases (e.g. for 3rd applications or standardized, transactional reporting). Moving to the right side, we see an increase in the levels of user interaction, statistical and analytical data processing and interpretation. Artificial Intelligence (AI) is currently seen as the most promising discipline to make decisions and perform actions like humans. The first steps in this direction are already a reality because natural language processing and machine learning (often included under the umbrella of AI) are gaining more and more maturity.

3.2 SAP HANA native

The SAP HANA native approach is an architectural design which relies solely on components of the SAP HANA platform. This results in its own challenges, which we discuss at the end of this chapter. First, let's look at which of the reference architecture elements we can use in a basic example of this scenario (see Figure 3.3).

Compared to the overall reference architecture introduced in Chapter 3.1, this figure shows that SAP BW/4HANA has been removed completely, including the BPC embedded option. If you would like to continue using BPC embedded, you need to do it inside your SAP S/4HANA system.

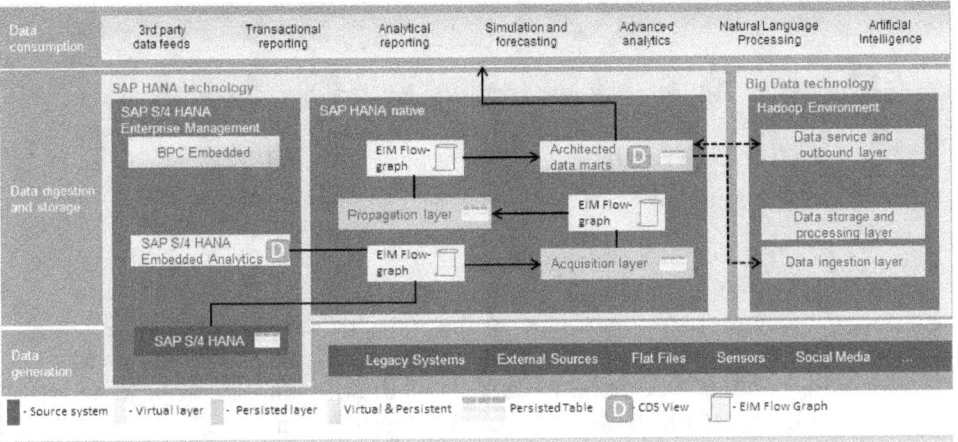

Figure 3.3: Reference architecture for an SAP HANA native scenario

3.2.1 The BI architecture

When designing your BI scenario in SAP HANA native, you might have to make some minor adjustments according to your requirements. Refer to Figure 3.3 for the general setup.

The landscape and its layers appear to be very simple. This can be misleading, because most companies have many flows leading into the acquisition layer. A simplification is on the way with SAP S/4HANA. We will deal with this specific problem, and how it can be integrated into your architecture, a little later. For now, let's look at the setup.

The **data generation** layer contains all the source systems. The SAP EIM option, with all its adapters, provides a particularly good solution for source system connections because many types of sources are supported. This includes: Hive, Google+, Apache Camel, Facebook, Twitter and real-time access (with some restrictions) to IBM DB2, Oracle DB, Microsoft SQL Server, and SAP systems. In the real-time sources from IBM, Oracle and Microsoft SQL Server, a log entry is first required before establishing the connections. Additionally, SAP S/4HANA offers Embedded Analytics (CDS views) which can be accessed easily via the SAP HANA real-time connection.

> **Real-time adapters for non-SAP sources**
>
>  The log reader adapters for real-time data access to Oracle, MS SQL Server and DB2 were introduced with SAP HANA 2.0 (December 2016) and significantly enhance the real-time capabilities of SAP HANA.

The SAP HANA Flow Graph enables users to add ETL steps between source and target. As discussed in the introduction of Section 3.2, we recommend keeping the functionality in the **data acquisition** layer to a minimum, because you need to capture all the data first in order to have historical data. When thinking about the future design of SAP S/4HANA applications, where CDS views will gradually replace the standard extractors, the extraction via SAP EIM is just as good as with SAP BW. Over time, this effect will become more obvious and will require the replacement of data flows. There are several additional advantages when using SAP EIM flow graphs to extract data:

1. Once the existing SAP extractors have been replaced by CDS views, you do not need to enhance the CDS views again to match the old extractors. Instead, you can use the logic built through SAP EIM and only use the CDS views when they offer a distinct advantage for your existing implementations.

2. Real-time data requirements can be handled well with SAP EIM because it offers many real-time connectors, including to SAP data sources.

3. A large number of non-SAP sources can be strongly supported through Smart Data Integration (SDI) connectors. This is especially helpful if, for example, your company previously only had 50% SAP source systems and covered the rest through other warehousing options such as Microsoft BI or the Oracle tool suite.

The SAP EIM solution also has several disadvantages which we discuss at the end of this chapter.

Most of the ETL operations take place between the **acquisition** and **propagation** layers. In almost all cases, the ETL processes are not as simple as the depiction in Figure 3.3. Instead, there are several connected data flows because data has to be transformed, merged or joined with other data, and several KPIs require calculations with data from several sources. The propagation layer then stores the converted data in the correct format. Compared to SAP BW, there are several points to consider when building your data model in SAP HANA directly, such as:

- SAP HANA offers a freedom in modeling your data that SAP BW does not. We will elaborate further on this in Section 3.2.3.
- Referential integrity is not automatically guaranteed in SAP HANA native. Developers are required to integrate these checks in the data model or the data flow.
- If checks on the data quality are requested by the business, then the path to the propagation layer is the best place to do this. The *data provisioning* functions offer help in that regard, which SAP BW does not directly supply. Here, SAP Smart Data Quality offers well-defined functionalities and out-of-the-box cleansing features (e.g. accuracy checks for address).
- The flow is modeled graphically (in most cases) and does not require ABAP knowledge, as is needed in SAP BW.

When coming from another BI area such as IBM, Oracle or Microsoft, these points will not apply. Instead, SAP HANA methods will seem natural to you.

The final layer in our reference architecture is the **architected data marts**. In our architecture, they are represented in tables and virtual constructs. Data mart tables store data grouped into specific business areas. There might, for example, be a set of tables with the same prefix or suffix containing all the information relevant for the finance area. These tables are then combined through SAP HANA views into one single output for reporting.

Virtual data marts

 Because SAP's current strategy involves the use of CDS views, we recommend modeling virtual data marts in CDS. However, calculation views are much easier to handle, but if SAP decides to no longer support calculation views, there will most likely be a migration path at a later time.

When constructing the virtual data mart, you should apply layering; first build an individual view for each table, then combine these views. However, be aware that each additional virtual transformation operation in these layers impacts performance and should therefore be kept to a minimum. If your propagation layer has already been modeled for maximum optimization (as suggested), and you only need a join between master and transactional data, then no further layers are necessary.

Finally, the path from the propagation layer to the architected data marts mainly involves the addition of some data mart-specific KPIs and characteristics, and the combination of additional data in order to minimize the number of joins and prepare the data for the data mart. Joins are very costly, even in SAP HANA, and should therefore be avoided. For further information on performance-impacting operations and recommendations, please see our book *SAP HANA Advanced Modeling*.

In the following sections, we look at the administrative tools needed to run an SAP HANA native architecture, including error handling, debugging, monitoring and job scheduling. Additionally, we discuss the integration with SAP Smart Data Streaming, Big Data platforms, SAP BW, and S/4HANA, as well as considerations for this architecture and the best time to leverage the SAP HANA native scenario for your company.

3.2.2 Administrative aspects

The XSA Engine, discussed in Chapter 2, is the administrative foundation of this architecture and is essential for running the SAP EIM add-on. The engine is not only used for modeling flow graphs in Web IDE form, but also enables developers to monitor jobs on the web interface. Additionally, the SAP HANA Data Warehousing Foundation offers features such as Data Warehouse Scheduler or Native DSO, similar to an ADSO in SAP BW (see Section 2.3).

Error handling, debugging and monitoring

After flow graphs have been modelled with one or more sources and targets, the flows can be activated and executed on Web IDE. If something in the flow does not work, an error message is displayed in the development environment. In recent years, debugging functionalities for SDI have greatly improved. With the Just-in-time (JIT) data preview, you can see your data during modelling. Figure 3.4 shows an example of the task monitor, displaying start times, end times, duration, status, and the number of rows that have been processed.

As you can see, the Data Provisioning Task Monitor is not as evolved as the SAP BW process chain monitor or other monitoring tools. However, clicking on the status (in the image, this is highlighted in green as "completed") enables the administrator to receive further information. For further enhancement of the monitoring and error handling functionality, we recommend the following:

- ▶ As with other BI tools, write your own tracking mechanisms with tables containing information such as rows read, rows written, rows deleted or updated, error messages from system tables, etc.
- ▶ For error tacking, consider creating your own views to get the information you need.
- ▶ In the algorithms, use case statements to handle faulty records. This assumes that you already know about data issues in advance.
- ▶ Therefore, import a subset of the (anonymized) productive data into your development environment in order to run sufficient tests for failures.
- ▶ Similar to SAP Data Services, template tables can be used for debugging if you are unsure where issues in the flow graph occur. In addition, SAP now offers Just-in-time (JIT) functionality to debug flowgraphs. When activating this feature for a certain transformation node, you are able to see the data in the node itself during development.
- ▶ Finally, construct check reports in front-end tools based on the views built by your developers in the backend; this enables better tracking of the data loads.

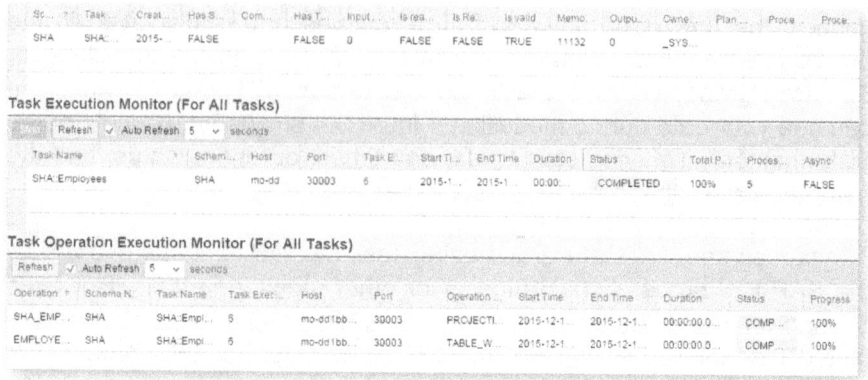

Figure 3.4: Data provisioning task monitor

Debugging

 The Just-in-time (JIT) functionality helps with viewing and debugging the output data of a node. In our practical tests with SAP HANA 1.0 SP 12, the JIT preview functionality did not always work as expected. Instead we recommend to use template tables for previewing / debugging your data.

Job scheduling

Tasks (e.g. SDI flow graphs) can be scheduled for execution via the Data Provisioning Task Monitor. This includes the possibility to define a frequency (e.g. daily) to the flow graph that is supposed to run recurrently. With the SAP HANA Data Warehousing Foundation, you can now also schedule task chains. This enables you to model dependencies between data provisioning tasks, similar to a process chain in SAP BW.

Task chain scheduler

 The task chain scheduler is required for all larger data warehousing projects in SAP HANA native and should be part of your solution. For further information, we recommend the following SAP help page: *https://help.sap.com/viewer/6d568ed106704106914ab3971505811d/2.0.2.0/en-US*

Data quality dashboards

As previously mentioned, error handling and job scheduling is more difficult than with SAP BW, but there are some extra features which can easily be implemented. One of them is data quality monitoring. The data can be gathered through SAP EIM flow graphs and combined in SAP HANA views for consumption in front-end tools. This is an advantage of using an SAP HANA native architecture.

3.2.3 General aspects

In this section, we look at points that need to be considered when designing an SAP HANA native architecture. This is by no means an exhaustive list, and your architecture may well have other specifics that arise from business requirements.

SAP HANA versus SAP BW

One of the most important aspects when coming from an SAP BW world is the freedom of design. In a data warehouse approach, whereby data models are handled completely by the developer and implemented directly on the database, the possibilities are endless. However, some aspects also need to be implemented from scratch. SAP BW has some restrictions compared to SAP HANA, but offers many out-of-the-box functionalities, and scores points for its integrity. Let's take a more detailed look at the advantages and disadvantages of an SAP HANA native architecture versus an SAP BW architecture:

► In SAP BW, the prominent objects for maintaining data on a physical level are the InfoObject and Advanced Data Store Object (ADSO). In SAP HANA, the data is stored in tables. Designers can choose how to model these tables, especially in regard to partitioning, relationships between tables, and general data models. This is particularly helpful for the propagation and data mart layer where an optimal data model results in better performance. If you want to model as freely as in SAP BW, while leveraging the full capabilities of an ADSO, please refer to the native datastore object (NDSO) information below.

- Directly related to this, is the option of a virtual data model. SAP HANA offers a much larger set of possibilities to realize data virtualization, compared to the CompositeProvider in SAP BW (e.g. aggregations, joins and calculations can be performed on the fly). However, keep in mind that SAP BW offers the functionally rich SAP BEx query designer as an additional component, which evens out the relative differences.

- The addition of data from subsidiaries with local customizations in their source systems is easy with SAP HANA. Data can be loaded quickly with SAP EIM and joined with the general data model (only if master data is being added). Local fact tables that need to be joined with the central KPI models are more difficult. In this case, a combined ETL flow needs to be created. This approach is similar to SAP BW.

- SAP HANA, with the SAP EIM option, does not support any metadata management when it comes to single data objects. SAP BW has InfoObject, which remains the same throughout a data flow and can be reused in other data flows. This option is not available in SAP HANA and developers need to use consistent names and data types throughout all flow graphs and tables in order to achieve a similar result. To give an example: if you have to model an object sales order, a column needs to have the same name, data format and size in each table in order for it to be consistent throughout the data warehouse. In SAP BW, this is easily achieved by reusing the same InfoObject.

- When using SAP HANA data models, developers have to handle referential integrity, surrogate keys and changes/updates during ETL. SAP BW automatically creates associations in the background and creates surrogate keys on the fly. This saves a lot of time during development, but also results in redundant surrogate keys; e.g. when the source system delivers these keys with the data model.

- Change and delta management is another SAP BW out-of-the box functionality. If no full load is required, then SAP BW automatically determines the recently-added rows and also automatically determines deltas in the target. A similar option is provided through NDSOs (see below for further details).

- From a governance perspective, SAP BW offers stronger restrictions (some things are impossible to do), whereas SAP HANA does not. Depending on your company and its established governance processes, this can be an advantage or a disadvantage. We discuss governance in more detail in Chapter 4.

- Most data flows, with any level of complexity, have to be designed in ABAP code or, with the new SAP BW/4HANA generation, in SQL code. The SAP EIM option offers a graphical modeling environment. So far, no in-depth studies have shown or confirmed whether one or the other is faster, but we can be fairly sure that that graphical modeling is learned much faster than coding. This is an advantage in a world where good IT resources are expensive, and resources that know how to create well-defined code are even rarer.

- Finally, the hierarchy support and out-of-the-box currency conversion in SAP HANA is lacking in functionality compared to SAP BW/4HANA. Therefore, it is still a good idea to integrate the SAP HANA virtual data model into SAP BW via Open ODS views. Another option is to provide the basic data model in SAP HANA and supply hierarchies via the front-end tool.

> **The native datastore object (NDSO)**
>
>  The native datastore object (NDSO) provides the invaluable ADSO, delivered in SAP BW, as part of SAP HANA native. The same options as in SAP BW are available for tracking change and generating historical data, and are delivered with the SAP HANA Data Warehousing Foundation. For further information, please visit:
>
> *https://help.sap.com/viewer/1e4f857a22aa477081d41d3b6fa48d99/2.0.2.0/en-US/10c100f55eb640c8ad71fdfd38ab4adf.html*

As you can see, there are many topics to consider when deciding on an SAP HANA native architecture. As already discussed, when coming from an Oracle or Microsoft BI world, these are standard topics usually handled by the development team and are not automatically handled via tools; an exception may be metadata management.

Tools related to an SAP HANA native architecture

SAP HANA native is the area in which SAP Smart Data Streaming (SDS) needs to be implemented, and we discuss this topic in this section. Although we do not recommend using the same SAP HANA Server for implementing SDS, it is still relevant for an SAP HANA native architecture. We will not cover the parallel use of an SAP HANA native data warehouse and SDS because of the excess load on the machine, resulting in crashes and/or long response times.

The operations that are performed with SDS should be implemented in a separate SAP HANA Server. The results can then be reused in your data warehouse either in SAP BW or SAP HANA, in an aggregated form. When the data needs to be further analyzed through SAP Predictive Analytics or the SAS Enterprise Miner, it makes sense to transfer the data to your SAP HANA native data warehouse. This data can then be merged with the data coming from your other data sources. We cover the predictive analytics options and architecture in more detail in Section 3.5.

Another advantage of an SAP HANA native environment over SAP BW is better support for Big Data connections. SAP Vora, Spark Controller, and other technologies can be leveraged to easily connect with a Big Data environment. For further information on this architecture option, refer to Section 3.4.

Finally, the external support of third party tools is in most cases better for SAP HANA than for SAP BW. SAP HANA offers a standard ODBC/JDBC interface to external and reporting tools, which simplifies data consumption.

3.2.4 Functional reasons for an SAP HANA native architecture

In the decision matrix shown in Section 3.9, we present relevant points to help you decide on the best architecture option for your needs. Let's now look at techno-functional and functional requirements that justify an SAP HANA native architecture:

1. Real-time requirements can be better met with an SAP HANA native architecture; the SAP EIM option (and Smart Data Streaming) offers far better support, compared to SAP BW.
2. If you have a large number of data sources, especially non-SAP data sources, an SAP HANA native environment connects very well to these.
3. Decentralized processes require a flexible data model and extensive ETL functionality. These can be implemented very easily with an SAP HANA native environment.
4. A data-insight-driven company needs flexibility in their data models, and a large number of options, to gather data and connect new data. SAP HANA connects well to Big Data platforms and can even be integrated with them in order to satisfy business needs for flexible and advanced data analysis. Additionally, predictive analytics functionality is combined with SAP HANA or a Big Data platform better than with SAP BW.

3.2.5 Advantages and disadvantages of SAP HANA native

We have outlined that a standard architecture in SAP HANA native is constructed with tables, the SAP EIM option and SAP HANA views. The data is loaded through three layers from the source system: the data acquisition layer, the propagation layer, and the architected data mart layer. We have also discussed administrative and general aspects of the architecture, which are summarized as advantages and disadvantages in Table 3.1

Discussion area	Advantage	Disadvantage
Design freedom	▶ High level of development freedom ▶ Optimized data model for better performance	▶ No metadata management in flows and tables ▶ Design freedom requires strict governance

Discussion area	Advantage	Disadvantage
Virtual data models	▶ Large number of options for virtual models ▶ Graphical modeling in calculation view enables development (with little extra knowledge required) ▶ Easy addition of master data from local subsidiaries, with their own data models	▶ Lack of experience can lead to data models with bad performance ▶ Less support of hierarchies and currency conversion compared to SAP BW
Graphical data / data flow modeling	▶ No coding knowledge required to create data flows in SAP EIM ▶ Out-of-the-box cleansing features (e.g. address checking) ▶ NDSOs offer change management features, like in SAP BW	▶ Creation of surrogate keys, and referential integrity needs to be handled by the developer (and not out of the box)
Error handling and debugging	▶ Error handling is rudimentary, but is possible through case statements or cleansing features in data flows. ▶ Gradual debugging while modeling via Just-in-time (JIT) data preview	▶ No easy error handling—some errors require in-depth analysis due to ambiguous error messages
Job scheduling and monitoring	▶ Out-of-the-box job scheduling and simple monitoring (SAP EIM) ▶ SAP HANA Data Warehousing Foundation Task Chain Modeler allows for modeling of dependencies ▶ Manual construction of monitoring dashboards by the developers can directly include data quality dashboards	▶ Advanced monitoring dashboards need to be constructed by the developers

Discussion area	Advantage	Disadvantage
Techno-functional aspects	▶ Good support of real-time requirements ▶ Large number of data sources and connections are supported ▶ Easy, agile development due to quick and easy graphical modeling possibilities, instead of heavy predefined development processes ▶ Good integration with third party vendor frontends, through standard ODBC/JDBC access	▶ No out-of-the-box extractors as with SAP BW (less relevant with CDS views)

Table 3.1: Advantages and disadvantages of an SAP HANA native architecture

As a result of these advantages and disadvantages, we recommend the following:

1. Use the SAP HANA Data Warehousing Foundation toolset when building an SAP HANA native architecture, in order to achieve better monitoring and create NDSOs for modeling.

2. You should initially define what monitoring information you would like to have. It is easy to include these in governance guidelines and architecture, but much harder to include them later on. If you come from an SAP BW world, it's best to work with people from an Oracle or Microsoft SQL Server environment.

3. Define a strict governance, and ensure that someone is responsible for all developments. It is very difficult to change incorrect field names later (for more detail, see Sections 4.2 and 4.3).

4. Use the features in SAP HANA, especially for agile development and the integration of local data models; you can really benefit from SAP HANA's strengths.

5. Consider using SAP BW on top of SAP HANA views, especially if you would like to use hierarchies. Currency conversion can easily be included manually in the SAP EIM flows; hierarchy handling can either be done in the frontend or delivered through SAP BW.

3.3 SAP BW/4HANA

In this section, we look closer at an SAP BW managed SAP HANA BI architecture. We consider SAP BW/4HANA to be the most advanced technology, leveraging SAP HANA features and capabilities from SAP BW. In doing so, we follow the given structure of the reference architecture, starting from source systems (data generation layer) via data transformation and persistency (data digestion and storage), to the area where end users or downstream tools utilize the data provided for their purposes (data consumption).

> **General information about SAP BW/4HANA**
>
>
>
> SAP's official release notes on the latest support package stacks are available at:
>
> *https://help.sap.com/viewer/b3701cd3826440618ef938d74dc93c51/1.0.8/en-US*

3.3.1 Data transfers

As described in Section 2.3, there are two ways to connect both SAP sources (via **ODP source system**) and non-SAP sources (via **SAP HANA source system**) to the SAP BW environment (in addition to a flat file interface):

ODP source system

Data transfers via the ODP framework can use either traditional Remote Function Call (RFC) connections to ABAP-based systems or web services based on Simple Object Access Protocol (SOAP) via HTTP/HTTPS; this includes systems not built on ABAP. In an ABAP environment, the RFC connection is still preferred due to its performance and effective communication. ODP supports various types of connectors to ABAP sources. You can use elements such as SAP extractors to leverage business content data sources (ODP—SAP (Extractors)), generic data sources, or connectors to other SAP BW systems (ODP—BW). Note that not all traditional data sources will be supported in SAP

BW/4HANA, so you need to check whether your specific extractor is ODP-enabled. New SAP HANA optimized content objects will leverage virtual models delivered by SAP S/4 Embedded Analytics, and therefore benefit from the CDS developments in your source system.

Depending on your architecture scenario, there are different options for connecting SAP repositories:

- SAP HANA database (with an ABAP system running on top)—ABAP CDS views can be accessed and used for the data transfer (ODP—ABAP CDS Views). However, delta and update mechanisms need to be defined by the developer (e.g. timestamp field). You need to contact SAP directly if you would like to use custom delta mechanism in CDS views in a productive solution.

- SAP Landscape Transformation Replication (SLT) Server via a delta queue, which provides the necessary deltas—The delta information can be pushed directly into an ADSO and the necessary delta operation is performed there (ODP—SLT Queue). Note: you can also leverage SLT for non-SAP database sources. Theoretically, you can also connect non-SAP sources via ODP.

- SAP Business ByDesign (ODP—SAP Business ByDesign) uses web service communication to replicate data to SAP BW (e.g. via analysis views). Only full extraction is supported (no delta queue support).

As a final note, existing SAP HANA information views (e.g. calculation views) can also be used as a source for data transfers (ODP—SAP HANA Information View).

> **Further information about ODP**
>
>  More details about data extraction via ODP is available at:
>
> https://www.sap.com/documents/2017/06/66673acb-c37c-0010-82c7-eda71af511fa.html
>
> and
>
> https://wiki.scn.sap.com/wiki/display/BI/Introduction+to+Operational+Data+Provisioning#IntroductiontoOperationalDataProvisioning-Purpose.

103

For a complete list of business content extractors currently available for ODP, see SAP Note 2232584—"Release of SAP extractors for operational data provisioning (ODP)".

Data Replication via SLT directly into InfoProviders

SLT provides near real-time capabilities to replicate data from SAP sources into a target system. With the ODP framework, the replicated data can be either loaded into the Persistent Staging Area (PSA) (using an InfoPackage) or directly transferred to an InfoProvider (using a Data Transfer Process). If you need semantic grouping, switch to data transfer via PSA. The SLT data replication approach also supports delta loads by making updates to the source tables available via a delta queue mechanism. SAP BW subscribes to the delta queue for further processing of the data.

As the SAP standard extractors are reworked and optimized for SAP HANA, the underlying table structures of an SAP S/4HANA system are thinned out. SAP currently offers no real strategic solution whether to stay on business extractors or switch to CDS views that are mostly not yet ready for productive use. Furthermore, many customers are dissatisfied with their complex, highly customized extractors and are looking for a new, transparent, and delta-enabled way to replicate their source data to SAP BW. You can check out further details on this option by visiting the following site:

https://help.sap.com/viewer/ccc9cdbdc6cd4eceaf1e5485b1bf8f4b/7.5.6/ en-US/6ca2eb9870c049159de25831d3269f3f.html.

SAP HANA source system

As described in Section 2.3, the SAP HANA source system connection type is positioned to access both non-SAP and non-ABAP-based sources by SAP BW. This approach leverages Smart Data Integration (SDI) for physical data transfers, and Smart Data Access (SDA) for remote access. Therefore, the established DB-Connect and UD-Connect source system types become redundant. Furthermore, the utilization of

SDI enables pre-processing and transformation of data before it enters the SAP BW environment. When retrieving data outside of a consolidated SAP scenario, this step is essential to validate the quality of the data.

> **Further information about SAP HANA source system**
>
>  All details about the SAP HANA source system connection type can be found at:
>
> https://help.sap.com/viewer/ 107a6e8a38b74ede94c833ca3b7b6f51/1.0.8/ en-US/4771b53a261c49ebb4de370bdbce2f29.html

For SDI, a large number of database adapters are available, building on JDBC connections. After the installation of the SAP HANA Agent, the deployment of a new adapter is more or less a copy of the respective JAR (Java Archive) file to a specified destination. Utilizing Java, you are also free to write your own database adapters.

> **SDI—supported adapters**
>
>  For a list of supported adapters, refer to Chapter 6 of the *SAP HANA Enterprise Information (EIM) Administration Guide*:
>
> https://help.sap.com/doc/dd356918159e4ba1a32927b0b91 7b78c/1.0_SPS12/en-US/SAP_HANA_EIM_Administration _Guide_en.pdf
>
> For more general information, go to: https://help.sap.com/viewer/p/HANA_SMART_DATA_INTEGRATION.

Some SDI adapters also enable a (near) real-time data replication via the SAP HANA source system. The replicated data can be used either via an Open ODS view or for updating to an advanced DSO. Note that the UPSERT subscription option always gives you the latest status of the data in the target table and INSERT provides you with the full history of delta data. The INSERT option enables delta updates to an advanced DSO using complete before and after images. Either option can be chosen, depending on your requirements and handling of delta updates.

105

> **Further information on real-time replication via SDI**
>
>
> Further information regarding data replication utilizing SDI can be found at:
>
> *https://help.sap.com/viewer/ ccc9cdbdc6cd4eceaf1e5485b1bf8f4b/7.5.9/ en-US/4ed3819b17aa41a5850031feb7bb40bf.html*

> **Connection of ETL tools**
>
>
> Classic ETL tools, such as SAP Data Services, and 3rd Party tools must also connect via SAP HANA source system.

3.3.2 Data Modeling

Not only have the connectors to ingest data into SAP BW/4HANA been consolidated and reworked, but the data modeling approach has also had noticeable changes. The LSA++ guidelines are still valid, but the difference now lies in how to design, setup, and follow them in real-life projects. Firstly, the type of objects available for data modeling have been consolidated and updated. As explained in Section 2.3, InfoObject, advanced DSO, CompositeProvider, and Open ODS view are the four core elements needed to build your system. Because the **acquisition layer** is mainly a persistent one, the advanced DSO (ADSO) is the key InfoProvider in this area (built on atomic InfoObjects and their combination. You need to consider the correct type of advanced DSOs for your specific data ingestion and delta update scenario. The acquisition layer is, in its baseline, the first entry layer into SAP BW, supporting fast and straight forward data ingestion (with only limited data transformations).

If you want to connect directly to an SAP HANA information view (and not follow the path through the source system and data source), then Open ODS view is a notable option. At a field-based level, you can access fields coming from SAP HANA information views and map them to InfoObjects (optional). The downside of Open ODS view is that structural changes in the source are not automatically forwarded to the dependent Open ODS view. You only notice changes during data loading when errors occur (when change management fails to inform downstream systems of changes in the source). In addition, the option of designing InfoProviders directly at field level requires additional considerations, as opposed to using predefined InfoObjects. You have to ensure that the right data type, right length, right conversion type, etc. is used for each field you manually define. Furthermore, it is your responsibility to ensure consistency across your landscape for each individual field

> **Modeling at a field-based level**
>
>
> There are both pros and cons to be considered when modeling your SAP BW InfoProviders at a field-based level. We highly recommend using the information in the following web page as a guide:
>
> *https://help.sap.com/viewer/107a6e8a38b74ede94c833ca3 b7b6f51/1.0.8/en-US/a348f4ca198a4e27bdb0eae72f7030cd.html*

The next layer, **propagation layer**, is an optional layer with a variety of flavors. From past experience on multiple projects, we have seen that in today's world, virtual enterprise data warehouses and the end of pre-transformations are still some steps away. The propagation layer is, therefore, the right place to store harmonized data and pre-calculated results which need complex, time-dependent operations on mass data. Physical storage, leveraging advanced DSOs, is mandatory in such a scenario. We believe that the propagation layer has various flavors because in our very heterogeneous world of reporting, analysis, and analytical requirements, not all calculations need to be additionally stored before being used. On one hand, the propagation layer is optional, and on the other, it is either physical or virtual (e.g. Open ODS view, CompositeProvider). The "veteran" concept of **architected data marts** is still useful to create projections on your data according to the specific needs of a user group or a data consumption tool (e.g. performance, governance, security). Simple architected data marts should be built only with virtual objects (mainly CompositeProviders as opposed to MultiProviders in earlier versions of SAP BW).

Following our suggested reference architecture (see Figure 3.2), we proposed the implementation of hybrid scenarios on this top most layer, enriching data marts with specific calculations implemented in SAP HANA. Alternatively, a hybrid scenario can also be implemented within the propagation layer. For implementation, we recommend the use of CompositeProviders (although there are known restrictions with these). In a hybrid scenario, for example, consider existing SQL procedures or SAP HANA Information Views which you would like to include in your SAP BW data model. A join or union operation with a CompositeProvider, based on the SAP HANA native object, is a simple solution and is a best practice for SAP BW/4HANA. However, exercise caution, especially when joining fact data in such a scenario.

Use of CompositeProviders

The use of CompositeProviders brings with it some constraints and restrictions that you have to consider upfront. CompositeProviders can currently only be transported when they consist solely of InfoProviders. It does not support cumulative key figures. Experience has also shown us that in certain cases, performance issues arise when combining mass data via CompositeProviders. Therefore, you should perform detailed testing of your specific usage scenario with CompositeProviders.

We recommend ABAP Managed Database Procedures (AMDP) for the inclusion of SAP HANA-based procedures or implementation of transformation logic, which can be pushed down to the SAP HANA database. AMDP can be implemented in SAP BW Transformations (e.g. start or end routine); native SQL or SQLScript can be used and existing SAP HANA objects can be leveraged. You can also access automatically generated SAP HANA views of advanced DSOs. The corresponding SAP HANA runtime object is created during the first execution of the AMDP. An additional advantage is the ease of transport via CTS.

> **ABAP Managed Database Procedures**
>
>
> For further details on ABAP Managed Database Procedures (AMDP), refer to the following SAP Help page:
>
> *https://help.sap.com/viewer/
> 6811c09434084fd1bc4f40e66913ce11/7.5.6/
> en-US/3e7ce62892d243eca44499d3f5a54bff.html*

Thanks to the in-memory power of the underlying SAP HANA database, multiple data transformation steps can now be implemented without storing costly interim results. From a data modeling perspective, the data logics can be grouped and sequenced via SAP BW transformation objects, which are connected via InfoSources. An InfoSource is a structured object without persistency, which you define based on InfoObjects in order to connect two transformations. By doing so, you can execute more than one transformation consecutively without (intermediate) data storage. However, due to performance and maintenance, best practice involves utilizing no more than two InfoSources between a source and a target InfoProvider. As mentioned earlier, it might still be necessary to store result sets as part of the propagation layer, depending on the complexity of the logic and the amount of data to be transformed.

> **Data layers in SAP BW**
>
>
> We have outlined the flexibility in designing the layers and options to virtualize your SAP BW data model. An illustrative representation of possible paths for moving your data through your SAP BW (and skipping layers for specific reasons) is given in the following blog:
> *https://blogs.sap.com/2016/09/07/data-modeling-with-bw4hana/*

With the launch of SAP BW/4HANA, we have seen a significant change in design and implementation of data flows. The transaction *RSA1* has been replaced by a **graphical data flow modeler** tool. The definition of data flows now requires SAP HANA Studio with the BW modeling perspective. This tool serves as the central point for designing and changing data flows end-to-end. It enables the compilation and connection of BW objects to a consistent data flow via drag and drop. With Data Flow Mod-

109

eler you can also directly enter the definition and customization pages of connected InfoProviders.

Although many functionalities have been moved to SAP HANA Studio, RSA1 and its relative transactions remain relevant. DataSource maintenance, process chain creation, authorizations, traces, and transports are still handled via SAP GUI. In addition, the SAP HANA web-based development workbench currently only supports SAP HANA native implementations (e.g. SAP HANA schema objects, SAP HANA information views). However, Web-based SAP BW administration has been planned.

Access SAP HANA web-based development workbench

The SAP HANA web-based development workbench can be accessed at:

http://<WebServerHost>:80<SAPHANAinstance>/sap/hana/ide/

Fundamental changes have occurred with regard to reporting and the definition of queries. The definition of queries in an SAP BW/4HANA scenario is performed in SAP HANA Studio via the BW Modeling perspective.

SAP Business Explorer maintenance and support policy

There are several implications regarding the support of Business Explorer, so we recommend reading the following blog:
https://blogs.sap.com/2016/10/13/sap-business-explorer-maintenance-support-policy/

SAP BW/4HANA—FAQ

SAP has published a document with key questions and answers regarding SAP BW/4HANA at:

https://www.sap.com/documents/2016/08/c4458a08-877c-0010-82c7-eda71af511fa.html#

3.3.3 Embedded solutions

With the rise of SAP S/4HANA, there is new momentum in the discussion about the split and location of transactional versus analytical reporting. In today's high-performance SAP HANA world, it is easy and reasonable to go back to the principle of having transactional reports at the place where data originates, without impacting daily business transactions. We have already talked about SAP S/4HANA Embedded Analytics, and CDS views and virtual models (see Section 2.2). Where transactional reporting needs more analytical functions, or if you want to benefit from SAP BW features (versus SAP HANA native implementations), you can enable SAP BW in an embedded SAP S/4HANA scenario. By doing so, you have a fully functioning SAP BW system utilizing your SAP S/4HANA system's resources.

We recommend a clear separation between such a scenario and enterprise-wide, harmonized reporting and analytic requirements. An embedded SAP BW scenario only makes sense for transactional reporting based on data arising in the same system environment. When adding foreign data, the amount should not exceed 25% compared to the overall amount of data within the SAP BW system. This follows SAP's recommendations, and in adhering to this threshold, you do not swamp or (over)load your business-critical SAP S/4HANA system with foreign data that you only occasionally need.

3.3.4 Benefits of SAP BW

When coming from an open, relational database world, creating data models in SAP BW can seem restricted and not very intuitive. However, having InfoObject as a reusable, granular element gives you one of the greatest benefits SAP BW has to offer: a highly **consistent data model**, across all layers, with master data stored only once but referenced multiple times. Furthermore, SAP BW comes with out-of-the-box functions for time-dependency, slowly changing dimensions, hierarchies, compounded keys, update rules etc. Since the early releases of SAP BW, developers have valued these features over self-programmed SQL or database scripts to ensure data model consistency and the correct handling of data updates. These fundamental SAP BW data modeling concepts have been implemented in the latest release.

Data loading, data handling, and data lifecycle management have gradually evolved into mature concepts. InfoProviders' request handling enables easy monitoring and correction of data loads. It is possible to schedule and monitor data flows via the graphical design of process chains. Restarting a failed process step exactly at the point of failure can be done in a process chain. Moreover, with SAP BW releases running on SAP HANA, data lifecycle has become much easier by leveraging the multi-temperature concept of hot, warm, and cold data. When storing warm and cold data, nearline storage solutions (NLS) such as Sybase/SAP IQ and Hadoop have become popular with SAP HANA-based SAP BW systems. The official SAP release notes (see tip box below) provide further information about the supported products and versions, as well as the functionalities.

With regard to authorization, SAP BW/4HANA continues the well-established, mature approach of previous releases. Access and data-handling rules can be defined from both an analytical and data perspective, fulfilling almost every requirement, including matrix requirements. Creating definitions is easily done with wizard and graphical support.

The Analytic Manager is a separate engine, processing and analyzing data during query runtime. It provides OLAP and planning features (Integrated Planning). The Analytic Manager is a rich tool for preparing data for the data consumption layer. Its support for enhanced business semantics, such as inventory key figures, stock cover reports, and elimination of internal business volume is valuable for many query requests.

SAP BW/4HANA—further details

 For the latest information about SAP BW/4HANA and its respective features, go to the official SAP help pages at: *https://help.sap.com/viewer/p/SAP_BW4HANA*. Features of the Analytic Manager can be found at:

https://help.sap.com/viewer/0cd8f518d3144ff4a4aecb3a7e5c097a/1.0.6/en-US/7679bf23cb214923abfc99ebe6423656.html

3.3.5 Migration to SAP BW/4HANA

Migrating to a new version of SAP BW always involves many prerequisites, and a lot of pre-migration and post-migration work. For an upgrade to SAP BW/4HANA, there are various ways to approach the new release. In general, SAP distinguishes between:

- new installations (greenfield approach),
- system conversions, and
- Landscape Transformation.

Migration paths to SAP BW/4HANA

To determine the right approach for your migration scenario, please follow the explanations in the blog "The Road to SAP BW/4HANA" at: *https://blogs.saphana.com/2016/09/07/the-road-to-sap-bw4hana-part-1/*. In addition, we recommend reading the SAP BW/4HANA master guide, available at: *https://help.sap.com/viewer/4500354f24f341408cf6af911f379e49/1.0.10/en-US/eb9490ff72ee4d919dc583a293c388df.html*.

In general, SAP BW 7.5 SP4 is needed to enable the SAP BW/4HANA mode. SAP has released some helpful notes which assist you to check whether your SAP BW (on HANA) system is ready for this switch, and which help you to perform the steps necessary to enable the SAP BW/4HANA mode.

Prerequisites—SAP BW/4HANA mode

Please refer to the following SAP notes when checking your system readiness for the SAP BW/4HANA mode (requires an authorized SAP user login):

- SAP Note 2285440 – Technical prerequisites in BW for "SAP BW Edition for SAP HANA" add-on
- SAP Note 2361350 – B4H mode: transport check for RS_B4HANA_CHECK_ENABLE
- SAP Note 2283111 – "SAP BW, edition for SAP" SAP HANA add-on – B4H mode

As a general condition, all objects have to be HANA-optimized. SAP BW 7.5, powered by SAP HANA, provides an "SAP BW/4HANA Starter Add-On" with migration tools. However, for older versions of DSOs and InfoCubes, run transaction RSMIGRHANADB to make sure InfoCubes and DSOs are HANA-optimized. This transaction code enables you to convert entire data flows. In addition, InfoObject catalogs are no longer supported and have to be migrated to InfoAreas by executing program RSDG_IOBJ_IOBC_MIGRATE_TO_AREA.

Automatic migration of SAP BW objects

From our experience on previous SAP BW upgrade projects, we strongly recommend thoroughly testing and checking the results of the automated migration routines. In case of abnormality, consider a manual migration of the particular objects.

Support of SAP BW add-ons

Not all add-ons are currently supported when switching to SAP BW/4HANA and you might need to uninstall them. SAP BPC 10.1 is supported, but special conditions apply. Check out all the relevant details in SAP Note 2189708—"SAP BW/4HANA Add-On Handling and Usage". In addition, see SAP Note 2011192—"Uninstalling ABAP add-ons".

3.4 SAP HANA merged with Big Data

In today's business intelligence and analytics landscape, classic data warehouse approaches and concepts are only one part of the entire landscape. As BI architects and developers, we have to consider, in particular, Big Data and analytic concepts. This is also applicable to SAP-driven environments. On one hand, we need to follow market demand, and on the other, we have to take technological drivers into account. This section focuses on SAP HANA environments merged with Big Data ecosystems.

As highlighted in Section 2.7, both platforms have their own positioning and purpose. Big Data landscapes are analytically driven, processing mass data in a more lab-like approach. They offer cost-effective storage of poly-structured mass data. In contrast, typical SAP HANA usage scenarios build mainly on structured data for high-performance reporting and data analysis (in addition to additional features and packages for predictive analytics, text mining etc., which are currently not the main drivers for an SAP HANA implementation). Storing data in SAP HANA requires significant investment in hardware and licenses, which leads to higher costs per gigabyte than in a Big Data ecosystem.

The key objective of this book is to design future-proof, flexible, and high-performing SAP HANA BI architectures; we hypothesize that the full power of BI and analytics can only be leveraged by combining both worlds: SAP HANA and Big Data. In this section, we discuss notable approaches and technologies which enable interaction and cooperation between these two platforms. With regard to Big Data, we focus only on the prominent and popular Hadoop stack, which has proven integration solutions with SAP HANA.

3.4.1 Foundational integration scenarios

In the following points, we discuss possible integration scenarios:

- **Data federation** is the concept of running both SAP HANA and Big Data platforms as equal content partners, providing each an almost incoherent range of data. Where mass and poly-structured data are involved, SAP HANA is economically and technically at a disadvantage compared to Big Data technologies. Data federation makes use of the strengths of each platform, particular to the volume and type of data. In this way, the transfer of physical data between the platforms is minimized. Data consumption (e.g. from reporting or analysis front-end tools) occurs via remote access to the other platform. Therefore, either one can be the leading technology, regardless of whether the report is built directly in SAP HANA or in Big Data. Data federation can also be supported by front-end tools (e.g. Tableau, Qlik) or the SAP Universe Designer. For a visual representation of data federation, see Figure 3.5.

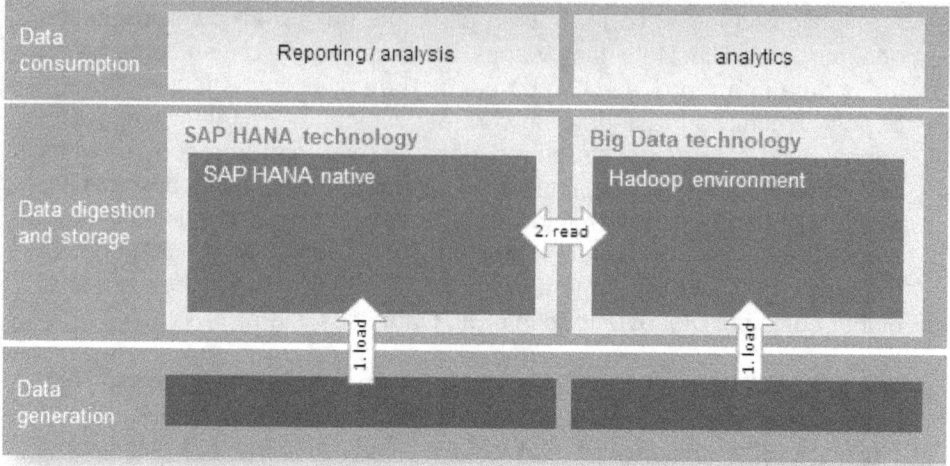

Figure 3.5: SAP HANA—Hadoop integration: data federation

- **Data aging** is the concept of keeping only data with the highest contribution or value for online reporting, and analyzing tasks in the SAP HANA database. Historical data is typically only accessed randomly. The data split is mostly performed via a time characteristic. Data older than a given point in time is physically moved to the more cost-effective Hadoop environment. However, data in both platforms remains online and available for reporting (analogue to data federation). Both push and pull approaches are technically possible, but in our experience, the concept works best when SAP HANA leads and coordinates moving the data to the Big Data world. As a side note, this scenario only makes sense when you already have a Hadoop cluster, or have solid plans to install one. Otherwise, you can look into data aging solutions; for example, with Sybase IQ. For a visual representation of data aging, see Figure 3.6.

SAP HANA BI ARCHITECTURES

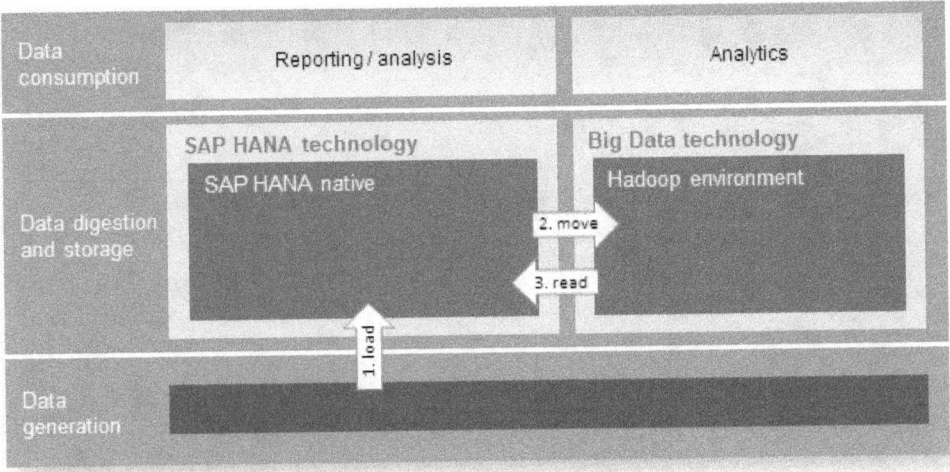

Figure 3.6: SAP HANA—Hadoop integration: data aging

- **Data lake** has been a widely discussed concept for years. From an SAP HANA BI architecture perspective, it is gaining new momentum as a central storage for all kinds of enterprise-related data. It is often called "Corporate Memory". This data can be originated internally and acquired externally, and can be of any type. In connection to SAP HANA, a data lake can act as a source for SAP HANA-based reporting and analytics applications by providing aggregated or pre-processed data. The data is either copied to SAP HANA for further preparations or accessed during on-the-fly query execution (Step 2). More and more customers are following this concept to quickly connect new data sources, or changed source structures, to their analytics environments (data lake), or to use Hadoop technology for pre-processing data. However, the reverse is also possible and is often implemented; analytics results and data from the SAP HANA BI world are transferred to the data lake. For a visual representation of a data lake, see Figure 3.7.

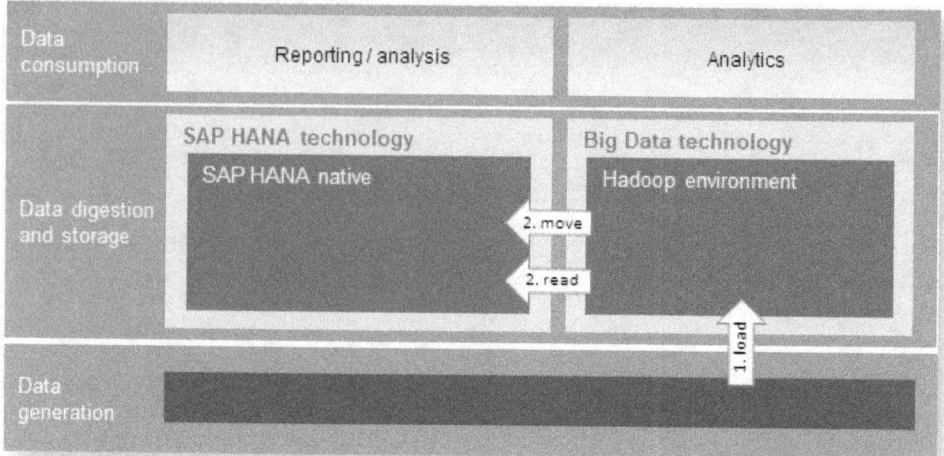

Figure 3.7: SAP HANA—Hadoop integration: data lake

3.4.2 Physical versus virtual connections

Looking at our reference architecture, we distinguish three layers on which a combination of SAP HANA and Hadoop is useful. At the bottom, physical data transfers should be implemented between the propagation layer (SAP HANA) and the data storage layer (Hadoop). In specific cases, transferring data from the acquisition layer (SAP HANA) is also an option, which we see as data aging. In most cases, taking data from the Hadoop space into SAP HANA also directly targets the propagation layer; i.e., data lake scenario.

In a data federation scenario, you should implement virtual remote connections between the architected data mart layer in SAP HANA and the outbound layer in Hadoop. For reporting/analysis purposes, data aging and data lake scenarios also require a virtual remote connection on the same layers. Of course, other implementation variants may also be valid here, depending on the use case.

Finally, a virtual remote connection can also be simulated in the data consumption tool (e.g. reporting tool). Some tools offer the possibility to consume data from several sources, and are therefore valid options for use in data federation and data aging scenarios (e.g. SAP BusinessObjects via Universe Designer). Figure 3.8 illustrates these options of combining solutions built with Big Data or SAP HANA technology.

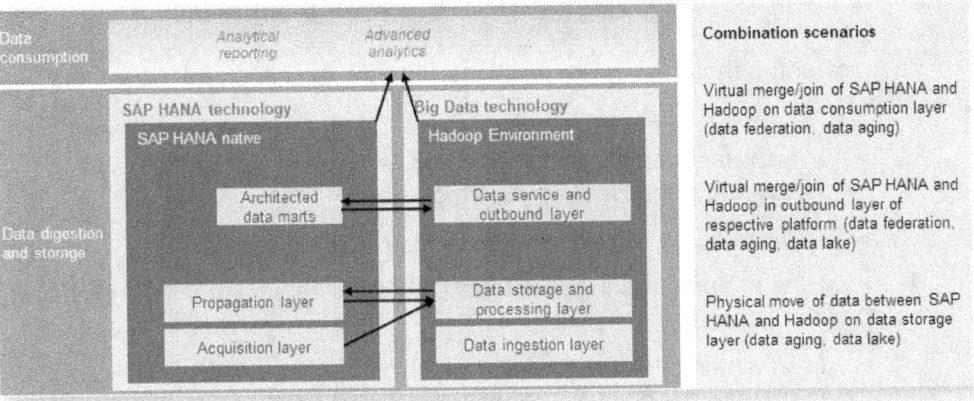

Figure 3.8: SAP HANA—Hadoop combination scenarios

3.4.3 Architectural considerations

When implementing any of the listed integration scenarios (or variations of them), many architectural questions and challenges arise. You first need to decide whether to use a Big Data environment at all. To assist you with this fundamental question, we have added a decision matrix at the end of this chapter (see Section 3.9). Regarding the scenarios presented here, we recommend you consider the purpose and guiding principles of your integration scenario:

- ▶ What is your specific integration scenario for and what objectives should be fulfilled?

- ▶ What are the reporting/analytical reasons for running an SAP HANA system? What are the reporting/analytics reasons for running a Big Data cluster? Is there a master system for your reporting/analytical demands?

- What use cases would you like to implement and what are their integration requirements? Are there real-time, or near real-time, SLAs to be fulfilled? How often will these integrated queries be executed?

- What is the minimum data which needs to be transferred between the platforms? Is there a need to transform or enrich the data when gathering them from the respective platform?

In answering these simple questions, further architectural questions arise:

- Which technological components are best for bringing SAP HANA data and Hadoop data together?

- Is a virtual/remote access possible or even needed?

- How are updates triggered from the other BI source (SAP HANA or Hadoop)?

- In which architecture should I establish the connection? Which is the right entry point to collect the required data?

- Where do I put the necessary transformation covering functional and technical logic?

These are just an example of the types of questions you need to address. To give you an idea of what has to be considered when implementing one of our integration scenarios, and how to set it up, we have compiled some basic statements and building blocks, as shown in Table 3.2.

3.4.4 Comparison of integration scenarios

Let's compare the integration scenarios based on their typical uses, associated technologies and expected benefits:

Criteria	Data federation	Data aging	Data lake
When to use	▶ when data comes from various sources in different formats (structured or unstructured) and arrives via various channels (e.g. ETL/ELT, streaming) in either SAP HANA or Hadoop	when you want to: ▶ keep only the most relevant data in SAP HANA, ▶ minimize the amount of data in SAP HANA, and ▶ leverage the Big Data environment for cost-effective data storage	▶ when building a central data storage point (e.g. corporate memory) considering data of various types and for multiple processing purposes
Common use cases	▶ reporting/ analysis scenarios, combining data from both worlds during query execution ▶ mutually enrich data from either Hadoop or SAP HANA (e.g. IoT sensor data on Hadoop combined with SAP S/4HANA master data)	▶ only the most recent data available in SAP HANA for high-performance reporting/ analysis (i.e. hot-cold / dynamic tiering) ▶ historical data still needed online, but longer access time is acceptable	▶ central (company-wide) data point to support various data usage scenarios (e.g. data analytics, classic data warehouse reporting)
Key architectural considerations	▶ virtual remote access for direct reporting/ analysis scenarios without data transformation logics ▶ physical data transfer for data enrichment scenarios; necessary data transformations should be implemented in the tool, which transfers the data from the source—update triggers can be organized as either push or pull	▶ physical data movement to meet the data aging requirements (without any data transformations) ▶ virtual remote access for overarching reporting (e.g. current data from SAP HANA and historical data from Hadoop platform)	▶ physical data transfer (copy) to SAP HANA; data transformations can be performed in the tool, which transfers the data, or in the definition of the Hadoop Outbound Layer itself (i.e. the Outbound Layer reflects the structure of the SAP HANA Inbound layer; data transfer follows only 1:1 mappings) ▶ the reverse also works in a scenario where SAP HANA BI system feeds the Data Lake

Criteria	Data federation	Data aging	Data lake
Core technologies	▶ SDA, Spark Controller, SAP Vora for remote (reporting) access ▶ ETL/ELT tools for physical data transfers from Hadoop to SAP HANA (e.g. SAP Data Services, SAP HANA Smart Data Integration (SDI), Informatica, Sqoop)	▶ ETL/ELT tools for physical data transfers from SAP HANA to Hadoop (e.g. SAP Data Services, Informatica, Sqoop) ▶ SAP Data Lifecycle Manager (HANA dynamic tiering option) ▶ SDA, Spark Controller, SAP Vora for remote (reporting) access	▶ ETL/ELT tools for physical data transfers from Hadoop to SAP HANA (e.g. SAP Data Services, SAP HANA Smart Data Integration (SDI), Informatica, Sqoop) ▶ SDA, Spark Controller, SAP Vora for remote (reporting) access
Technology learnings	the best experience when combining the two worlds was with: ▶ SAP HANA leading and merging/joining the data in calculation/CDS views (after reading data from Hadoop via Spark Controller/SDA), and ▶ executing the merge/join on the Hadoop side, leveraging Spark and SAP Vora to gather SAP HANA data ▶ the combination of data in the frontend is only useful when a small amount of data is collected on both sides	▶ from previous projects, we see benefits in using mature ETL/ELT tools to transfer data bi-directionally between the platforms ▶ the Data Lifecycle Manager demonstrates good wizard-based capabilities to easily set up and run data aging scenarios. ▶ alternatives such as JCo, SQLScript plus SDA require more programming and maintenance effort	▶ data lake scenarios may also need a write back to the Hadoop cluster. ▶ it is recommended to use the same data transfer technology for inbound and outbound connections. ▶ for loading or replicating structured source data into the central data lake, technologies such as Change Data Capture (CDC) or SAP System Landscape Transformation (e.g. in combination with SAP Data Services) are valid approaches

SAP HANA BI ARCHITECTURES

Criteria	Data federation	Data aging	Data lake
Benefits	▶ reduction of TCO by leveraging Hadoop as cost-effective storage and pre-processor of data (no additional copy of reporting relevant data to SAP HANA) ▶ leverage Hadoop's processing power to handle mass data, structured or unstructured	▶ reduction of TCO by leveraging Hadoop as cost-effective storage and, in turn, saving SAP HANA hardware and license costs ▶ queries accessing most recent data only run on a reduced amount of data in SAP HANA, and are therefore faster and generate less load on SAP HANA	▶ reduction of TCO by leveraging Hadoop as cost-effective storage and massive parallel processor of data ▶ new, enriched reporting/analysis scenarios based on proprietary structured data from transactional sources combined with insights gained from unstructured data in Hadoop
Best Practice	▶ Following the best fit idea, data is managed, processed, and stored separately in the respective target only (SAP HANA or Hadoop), based on the type of source and its structure. ▶ Utilize the *core technologies* of the leading platform to establish data connections.	▶ According to the business SLAs, data from last year, plus the current year to date, is kept in SAP HANA; accepting latency in reporting, older data is accessible in the Big Data environment following the data federation approach.	▶ Benefiting from cost-effective handling and storage of large amounts of data, central data lakes based on Big Data technologies are popular for building corporate memories. These act as sources for numerous kinds of data consumption tools and methods.

Table 3.2: Comparison of foundational SAP HANA - Hadoop integration scenarios

The SAP Data Lifecycle Manager (DLM) is a highly promoted tool for data aging scenarios and has some promising features. The key elements of DLM are summarized in the following:

> ### SAP Data Lifecycle Manager (DLM)
>
>  The SAP HANA dynamic tiering option of the SAP Data Lifecycle Manager (delivery unit HCO_HDM_DLM of the SAP Data Warehousing Foundation) enables simple set-up of data relocation scenarios. Data lifecycle profiles enable you to determine the point at which you want to move data from hot to warm/cold storage. The rule editor then enables the definition of SQL-like filter criteria to select the correct datasets for the relocation. The execution is triggered either manually/directly or via a schedule. Automatically-generated pruning and union views, as well as relocation database procedures, enable general access or control from outside the DLM environment. DLM works bi-directionally. Further information can be found at:
>
> *https://blogs.sap.com/2017/03/16/hana-data-warehousing-foundation-dwf-data-distribution-optimizer-ddo-and-data-life-cycle-manager-dlm/*
>
> and:
>
> *https://assets.cdn.sap.com/sapcom/docs/2016/06/faa2e425-777c-0010-82c7-eda71af511fa.pdf.*

3.4.5 Challenges

Even though the integration of SAP HANA and Hadoop is possible at a technical level, there are still challenges you have to deal with when taking this promising integration approach:

- ▶ **Technological integration components**—There are many ways to transfer data from SAP HANA to Hadoop, and vice versa. New and existing tools have been enhanced to provide appropriate interfaces and functionalities. However, these tools and features are still evolving and are sometimes quite immature, or they impose many restrictions and limitations. We therefore turn to the supported Hadoop versions from SAP HANA. Finding the right version of the required connector can be like finding a needle in a haystack. Additionally, there is currently not a lot of experience in productive environments and little knowledge on the scalability of components such as SAP Vora. This poses a risk requiring mitigation through proof of concept and comprehensive testing in your specific scenario.

- ▶ **Technological characteristics**—Another characteristic which needs to be taken into account is latency when running combined reports (i.e. reports querying SAP HANA and Hadoop in parallel). SAP HANA is very good at answering structured (SQL) queries, and Hadoop's strength lies in its ability to analyze all kinds of data. Hadoop is not built to select a specific small set of data within the petabyte of data stored in the cluster. A huge overhead in data processing arises when trying to identify specific records/values, which leads to delays in query response times. We could easily demonstrate this in integrated scenarios using SDA with Hive or SAP Vora. Depending on the scenario, the installation of an additional database, such as HBase or Cassandra, could be useful to provide a fast key-value store.

- ▶ **Authorization**—There is currently no seamless integration of authorization concepts available. You could start with the Lightweight Directory Access Protocol (LDAP) or Active Directory, which both worlds can connect to. SAP authorizations could be extracted from system tables, transforming the technical structure and importing basic rules to the Hadoop ecosystem (e.g. Apache Ranger). However, the question arises whether there is really a need for an overall authorization concept (will the same user groups work separately in both worlds?).

- ▶ **Data loads** (end to end)—This is a key issue, especially in the data lake scenario. Which tool enables end-to-end control and monitoring of the data load chain? In cases of delta load failures, the correct data pointer needs to be identified for the restart. Finding the right solution (tool support) for this issue is especially tricky at the edges of the platforms, when data is about to leave one world and enter the other. Classic concepts of sequence identifiers or timestamps can help to overcome this issue.

- ▶ **Synchronization of developments**—This is an ongoing issue, well-known from many other distributed development scenarios. The key issue in our integration scenarios is the alignment of changes (e.g. structural enhancements) between the SAP HANA and Hadoop development teams. Continuous integration and continuous deployment approaches can help to quickly identify changes impacting the other party.

- **Metadata management**—It is crucial to centrally supervise and maintain metadata along the entire data path, in order to achieve high data quality. There are tools available (e.g. SAP Information Steward or Informatica Big Data Edition) which provide the necessary functionality to investigate and visualize metadata end-to-end in an integrated SAP HANA and Hadoop scenario.

- **Historization of data**—Building an accurate history of records, as in a data warehouse solution, can be very challenging in a Big Data platform. For example, if you want to see the address history for one customer in the report, actually storing the history, so it can be used in that way, is challenging in file-based storage. The problem here is that files are usually only appended and do not have primary keys, therefore finding the last record of a certain customer is very hard.

- **Transactional consistency of data**—Ensuring transactional consistency of data in a Big Data platform requires additional implementation effort. This is due to the fact that Big Data platforms follow the BASE principle (i.e. Basically Available, Soft state, Eventually consistent). That means that the Big Data platform is at some point consistent, but this is not guaranteed while data is being ingested.

3.4.6 Drivers and benefits

We have learned about specific characteristics and challenges of integration scenarios, and now we would like to highlight the key benefits of combining SAP HANA and Hadoop.

There are three key drivers supporting the integration of SAP HANA and Big Data platforms:

- **Reduction of total cost of ownership (TCO)**—It is possible to move data seamlessly into the Big Data storage environment (e.g. data aging scenario), where it is not absolutely necessary to store it in the expensive SAP HANA in-memory space. Furthermore, there is still a need to reduce hardware and license costs; organizations try to avoid limiting themselves to a single vendor.

- **New reporting and analytics use cases**—Both platforms have different focus areas for data analysis. Big Data technologies are the frontrunners for analyzing all kinds of data, and are therefore often the basis for lab environments and are the preferred platforms for data scientists. SAP HANA, on the other hand, enables high-performance analysis on structured data. In connecting both technologies, you also combine their strengths in data processing and open new doors for data analysis (e.g. when combining company-originated, structured data with unstructured data from social media platforms in one report).

- **Future-proof architecture**—On one hand, core SAP software components run on SAP HANA (or they will in the near future). On the other hand, the tremendous potential of Big Data technologies is being recognized by many organizations. Analysts, such as Gartner, foresee the merging of various data analysis approaches into a holistic data and analytics discipline with end-to-end architectures, across all levels of an organization (see also the Gartner blog "2017: The Year That Data and Analytics Go Mainstream"). Looking at the core theme of this book and transferring technology trends and market perceptions to SAP HANA BI architectures, it becomes clear that a modern, future-proof architecture encompasses SAP HANA and integrates it with other strong players in the analytics field, such as Big Data, into one powerful unit. From this, various reporting and analytics disciplines are possible (e.g. classic reporting, data analytics, machine learning, and artificial intelligence).

Our experience with project work and workshops, our discussions with clients, and feedback from market analysts confirm the importance of an integrated, end-to-end BI architecture.

New technology trends form and foster new use cases which further drive demand for SAP HANA-Hadoop integration (e.g. IoT and streaming cases which process large amounts of sensor or machine data in Hadoop and linking exceptions with transactional/process data in SAP HANA).

3.5 SAP HANA merged with analytics

With the right tools and technologies, predictive analytics can be run on any architecture and, in principal, in any environment. SAP HANA, with its in-memory capabilities, offers the unique possibility of combining and integrating your predictive analytics scenarios into your company's data warehouse.

Many predictive analytics projects are started on a new system, with a select copy of productive data, and often with a limited memory and calculation power. This is reasonable when implementing an initial use case to prove benefits and demonstrate general functionalities. However, this approach does not work long-term, when models need to be transported to a productive landscape for training and constant monitoring. Here, it is necessary to have a complete system line, with a development, test and production environment. There are proprietary solutions from the predictive-analytics software vendors, but there is also the option to leverage the calculation power of your hybrid architecture. When integrating a predictive analytics solution into your environment, there are three options to consider:

- **Solution 1**—Integrate the predictive analytics software with the SAP HANA database and leverage the in-memory capabilities of SAP HANA, and possibly reuse existing data warehouse structures.
- **Solution 2**—Construct the predictive analytics software on your Big Data solution.
- **Solution 3**—Use a hybrid approach of (1) and (2) above.

In the following sections, we will not only discuss the general architecture for predictive analytics scenarios, but also detail how to integrate these implementations with your Big Data or data warehouse platform.

3.5.1 Architectural setup

The biggest difference between typical data warehouse or Big Data projects lies in the way the final data model has to be built. Statistics generally require a **wide format**, which means that for one evaluation object, all data needs to be in one row.

> ## Wide format
>
>  Imagine a typical customer analytics project in which you aim to find out more about your customers and identify important factors for customer retention or sales. One such factor could be salary, which most companies will not know, but which can be estimated by looking at customers' home addresses (i.e. rich or poor neighborhood), the average monthly sales volume per month generated by customers, the items they buy, etc. For this type of analysis, the dataset has to consist of the customer's address, the average value of the items bought in a given year, and the average annual sales volume generated by them, in one row. Figure 3.9 compares a typical data warehouse table structure with the wide format.

Customer ID	Customer name	Average sales volume per month	Minimal sales volume p.m.
1	Dominique Alfermann	62.20 €	17.70 €
2	Stefan Hartmann	76.90 €	35.60 €

Predictive Analytics

Data Warehouse

Product table

Product ID	Name	Price
1	Soap	8.90 €
2	Water	5.90 €

Fact table

Sales ID	Product ID	Customer ID	Quantity	Date
1	1	1	5	2017/12/01
2	2	1	3	2017/12/06
3	1	2	4	2017/12/15
4	2	2	7	2017/12/18

Customer table

Customer ID	First name	Last name
1	Dominique	Alfermann
2	Stefan	Hartmann

Figure 3.9: Comparison of data warehouse format to the wide format used in predictive analytics

The wide format usually necessitates decisions by the developer; for example, which address should be used when a customer has changed their address during the year? For normal data warehouse reports, these questions can also arise, but far less frequently.

A further point specific to predictive analytics is the time required for data preparation. A rule of thumb is that approximately 90 % of effort should be spent on data preparation and 10% on actual statistical modeling. This mostly involves amending data into the wide format, but also solving data issues, such as duplicates.

Having discussed the specifics of preparing data for predictive analytics scenarios, let's now look at the predictive analytics architecture for an SAP HANA native based predictive analytics solution (Solution 1 above), as depicted in Figure 3.10.

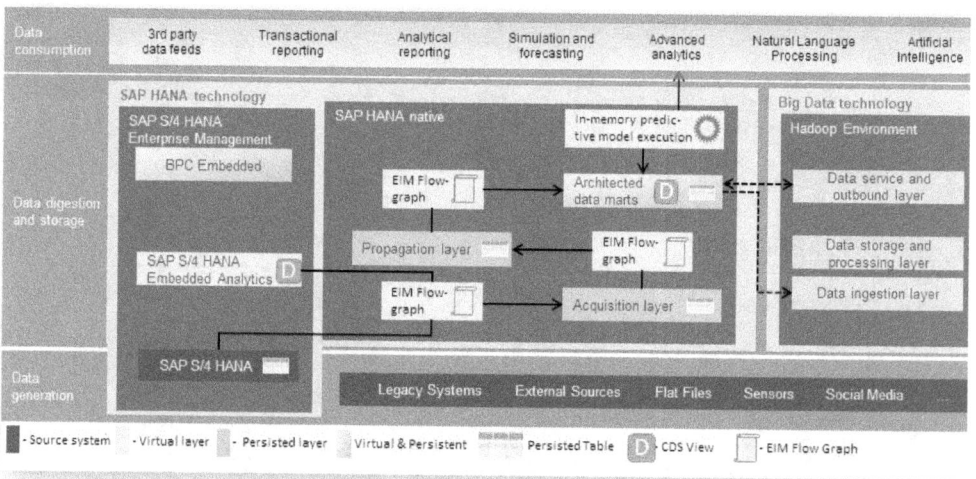

Figure 3.10: Simplified SAP HANA advanced analytics architecture (example)

Over the last few years, many projects have built their own cleansing flows directly in the predictive modeling tool, without architectural considerations. Additionally, governance aspects (e.g. for handling data inconsistencies) have been handled only in the tool itself and not at the appropriate organizational levels. Analytics projects usually result from highly pressing business questions driven by the business, and the IT department is not always aware of all the variations and effects of an analytical scenario. (We discuss this organizational issue in more detail in Section 4.2). One long-term option here is to push down the data preparation to the SAP HANA platform and use SDI flows to prepare the data. We discuss this option in more detail later within this chapter.

Depending on your chosen scenario, another option is to execute the predictive analytics model on your Big Data platform (Solution 2, defined above). Support for offerings in this area has grown in recent years. IBM, for example, offers advanced analytics models in combination with their InfoSphere streams software, and connectors to the Big Data platform. However, when working with large amounts of data, only using connectors to software environments may not be enough. Instead, a code execution within the Big Data cluster may be necessary. Such a code push-down is offered by SAS.

Finally, in a hybrid scenario (Solution 3), data is used from both platforms and then generally requires its own server to execute the predictive analytics model. You could push down the model execution into SAP HANA, but then the question arises—why not execute the model directly in your SAP HANA environment and use an SAP SDA connection, for example, if you do not want to store your data? This scenario is useful, if you do not want to transfer data between your Big Data platform and SAP HANA, but need to use data from both environments. For example, combining weather data analysis results with your planned transportation routes in order to avoid missing parts in production.

SAP HANA native integration

One of the key drivers for integrating your predictive analytics solution with your existing SAP HANA-based solution (i.e. a data warehouse or S/4HANA), is the availability of productive data. In most SAP environments, productive data is only available on the production server, but not in the test or development environments. So, you may not be able to utilize the existing landscape when leveraging an SAP HANA native server line, be it in your S/4HANA server line or in your SAP HANA-based data warehouse for predictive analytics. There are three options:

1. Establish a new server line for the predictive analytics solution. However, the advantages of being able to push code into SAP HANA cannot be used with your existing servers, creating additional complexity in your landscape

2. Enable your test environments or develop environments to have productive data. This can be difficult if you have offshore development resources

3. Differentiate between three different environments in your predictive analytics tool, but in each environment always refer to the SAP HANA native productive server.

> **Using existing SAP HANA environments**
>
>  Before building a predictive analytics solution on existing environments, make sure your servers have the right sizing in order to cope with the additional load on the system.

The option of reusing existing SAP HANA native environments has the following advantages:

- There is little additional complexity through the predictive analytics solution.

- In the long run, code for the data preparation can be pushed back to the data warehouse processes (e.g. via SAP SDI) if your predictive analytics solution is based on an SAP data Warehouse.

- Results can be directly reused for further reporting when written back to the server, with existing reporting solutions connected on top.

- Further combination of data is possible (e.g. with the data warehouse data), in order to enhance reporting.

- You can reuse the existing possibilities for model push-down (e.g. via SAS or SAP Predictive Analytics, as covered in Chapter 2).

Big Data platform integration

In this scenario, the predictive model runs on the Big Data platform and in the best case, leverages the calculation power provided through the cluster. SAS, for example, offers a Hadoop push-down option. Let's look at the benefits of such a scenario:

- There is no limitation on the sizing. SAP HANA has limitations regarding its size, and Big Data platforms can be scaled up and out based on the existing demand.
- In the case of a data lake, you have access to a large amount of data; this is especially useful for data scientists who want to explore the data and a build statistical models on it.
- Large amounts of data deliver better training results for machine learning and predictive analytics models.
- You can leverage the productive data available on the test environments; large scale applications first need to be tested on large amounts of data before they can be deployed to production.

In general, Big Data platform integration is a good solution if you want to explore data and perform initial data explorations, including on unstructured data.

Hybrid predictive analytics solutions

As explained above, in hybrid scenarios, the predictive analytics solution uses both environments: the Big Data cluster and the SAP HANA data warehouse. This makes sense when no data needs to be transferred between the two environments; otherwise, you could just transfer all data into one environment and then run your model only on the one environment. Some possible solutions to avoid loading too much data into the predictive analytics server include:

1. Push down calculations to the Big Data or SAP HANA environment where models can be kept separate (e.g. for data preparation).
2. Limit your calculations to the data you really need.

> **Hybrid scenarios**
>
>  In general, we do not recommend this scenario because there is no real reason not to push all your data into the Big Data cluster or SAP HANA environment. If your statistical models run on large amounts of data, the Big Data cluster is the preferred option for storing all the required data.

3.5.2 Administrative aspects

Similar to data warehouses, predictive analytics platforms also necessitate a monitoring of deployed models and a transport system for moving models into productive maintenance. This topic was briefly introduced in Chapter 2 and we will now look at it in more detail.

Model management and optimization

There are several technologies which need to be applied in order to manage and optimize the created models. If models are going to be executed on the SAP HANA database directly, they have to be translated into coding compatible with SAP HANA. As discussed in Chapter 2, native SAP HANA database integration is mainly supported by the SAS Predictive Modeling Workbench for SAP HANA, and by SAP's own predictive analytics toolset. In addition, SAS supports a code push-down into the Big Data cluster. For SAS, there are the SAS/ACCESS technology components for data access, and the SAS Scoring Accelerator for the model translation into SAP HANA executable code. For SAP Predictive Analytics, the predictive engine is part of the platform, so models can be imported into both SAP Predictive Analytics and SAP HANA. Additionally, the integration of SAP HANA with the R server enables developers to use R in combination with SAP Predictive Analytics, or SAS when executing code in-memory. This SAS and R-based architecture has to be set up as outlined in Chapter 2.

For models to run productively, you need at least one development server and one production server; independent of whether the predictive analytics technology is based on the same system line as the BI environment or not (this is discussed in more detail in the next section). When changing, adjusting or enhancing models, this cannot be done on the productive server because it would inhibit models from running in parallel. The models need to be developed, tested and deployed. Productive data is required at all times for comprehensive data scientist work, so the development environment has to be a complete copy of the productive server and has to be sized accordingly (although for less users). Therefore, a two-system landscape or, where possible, a single productive server can save a lot of money, not to mention time, when granting access requests. In big companies in particular, access to productive data is very restricted.

With this in mind, let's look at how models are managed in predictive analytics tools such as SAS or SAP PA. The SAS Model Manager and the SAP Predictive Analytics Predictive Factory manage versions on the model server. As with Java eclipse, different versions of models can be kept and tested in order to improve the created program flows and correct mistakes. Developers then deploy the version onto the server as the productive version, once sufficiently tested.

On one hand, this enables comparisons between models; not only in regard to testing, but also according to statistical measures such as significance and relevance, for example. On the other hand, when dealing with one server only, models can be developed while having one model as a productive version. However, as mentioned before, this approach does not make sense if the server is already under duress or needs to be constantly available.

Scheduling and monitoring

In this section, we look at scheduling options for executing models, retraining, and other tasks involving monitoring. The set of functionalities varies depending on the tool. Both the SAS and SAP predictive tool suites offer suitable scheduling functionalities. For example, retraining and scoring can be done as a repeated activity and helps in evaluating how good a model currently is. The SAS Model Manager lets you define thresholds for which a model needs to be executed and also enables you to set alerts in case the model's statistical performance has degraded below a certain defined threshold. The same cannot currently be said for the SAP Predictive Factory, which seems to have evolved from the old KXEN and Infinite Insight solution and therefore only has limited support for custom models. You can schedule retraining and deterioration checks for models, but alerts via email are not possible.

Tasks such as retraining and deterioration checks are both examples of monitoring activities because you usually want to know whether a model is still reliable or not. You would naturally also want to know whether it was executed successfully. This depends largely on your own scenario. Consider the following example: batch execution A (where data is loaded, and the data is then run through a model) has to be monitored once a batch run is started. An on-demand execution B (e.g. a credit scoring scenario) gives results, or not, depending on the successful execution. Here, little monitoring is required because the business user probably registers a complaint if something does not work. Finally, we have execution C, in the case of streaming scenarios. In this case, constant monitoring is required. We will now focus on cases A and C and look at the monitoring capabilities.

The SAS model manager offers a cockpit to track the performance status of models, the degradation, and other factors. SAP also offers some capabilities in this area, but not to the extent that SAS and other established vendors have already developed.

Error handling and debugging

It is common to find errors in every data stream; for example, there are unexpected values in the data or certain required information is missing. In these cases, both SAS and SAP Predictive Analytics offer little help. Error handling is usually taken care of by the developer. There is no way to automatically exclude faulty records. Instead, faulty records require the whole dataset to be rerun if they are not identified and handled during runtime. SAS offers the possibility to include manual coding in the SAS generated code. SAP Predictive Analytics offers a limited capability whereby you can export the code in Predictive Model Markup Language (PMML) and edit it. However, adding manual coding to a system-generated code should be avoided, especially if the model changes due to new developments. Therefore, we recommend the following strategies:

- Wherever possible, perform data quality checks, directly in your data warehouse, during the data extraction process. This reduces the time needed for predictive analytics projects and improves data quality.
- When building models, first run a check to confirm that all necessary values are filled as expected. This may not be relevant for a trial model, but for a productive one, it can minimize problems in production. Identify incorrect data sets and store them in a table, with an error message, and process them after the model run.
- Debugging is mostly possible by executing the model up to a certain step. This is helpful when you suspect that a certain operation is causing the error.
- Avoid system-generated code alterations by any means possible.

3.5.3 General aspects

In the following section, we'll look more closely at the topics previously mentioned: integration with BI developments, data quality aspects, variable preparation, and last, but not least, integration with external data sources.

Data quality

The first outcome of a predictive analytics project often involves the discovery of data quality issues within the source systems; for example, fields are not filled out correctly, values are missing, or records for the same entity have two different values that should not exist. In turn, this leads to new initiatives for improving data quality. The integration of predictive analytics efforts with a data warehouse environment can be very helpful here. In many data warehouses, data quality issues have already been addressed and if not resolved, at least improved.

Identifying these problems means that a business is aware of the issues and eases the path to data quality projects.

Variable creation

Building statistical models is a crucial task and is often done by data scientists. It requires examination of the data and evaluation of the variables that do and do not deliver value. Categorical variables need to be split into numerical variables with values 1 and 0 for each category in order to create regression analyses.

> **Categorical variable split**
>
>  Imagine this scenario: you want to evaluate a person's food preference (e.g. vegetarian, fruitarian, Halal, Kosher or "normal"). Instead of having one variable for each of these categories, you require a variable for each category (theoretically you need n-1 categorical variables, but let's not get too detailed). So, you create a variable v_vegetarian which is either 1 (=vegetarian) or 0 (=not vegetarian).

With SAP HANA, one approach could be to implement these variables in SAP HANA or SAP BW, once they have been clearly defined, and then reuse them in future statistical tools projects. Most tools already offer an automatic variable split, but often the naming does not conform to company standards, or simply does not make sense (e.g. with numbered categories); so, you have to put in the effort to name these fields anyway.

External and unstructured data sources

Advanced analytics it is often referred to in conjunction with Big Data. External data sources deliver valuable information not only for predictive analytics, but also for normal business intelligence. Many companies use Nielson data[4] to enrich their customer data, and others work closely with government organizations (e.g. for credit scoring in the insurance industry). This data can be easily evaluated in a data warehouse when it comes in the right format. However, for unstructured data, initial algorithms (e.g. text mining) have to be applied in order to work with the data. This is most efficiently done in a Big Data cluster, which leads us to

---

[4] Nielson provides market research data on customer behavior. For more information visit http://www.nielsen.com/us/en.html

the crux of the matter—Exactly what data do you pull out of the data warehouse based on SAP HANA, and what do you have to analyze on the Big Data cluster? Technologies such as SAP Vora help to communicate and exchange data with the Big Data cluster (see also Section 3.4), but that does not eliminate the decision itself. Unfortunately, we have no clear recommendations for this, but we want to raise two points to consider while making the decision:

- What level of detail do you need? First and foremost, Big Data lakes contain replications of raw data. This may be interesting for an initial analysis, but data scientists soon find out which variables are important, and with what level of detail. We recommend first analyzing the data with your predictive analytics tool, then seeing if you really need the level of detail within the Big Data cluster, or if you can just use an aggregated extract.

- If you require large amounts of data with a high level of detail, it could make sense to load data from the data warehouse, or any other source, into the Big Data cluster (or a separate streaming server, if it is streaming data) and do all your analysis there. SAS, for example, supports connections to Big Data sources as well.

These are the two options you have. A third option is the combination of these two, but we do not recommend it. In large developments, switching between systems with your analytics tool leads to confusion, especially when you need a combination of data out of your Big Data cluster and your data warehouse.

3.5.4 Functional reasons for predictive analytics

Predictive analytics has long established its business worth and there are many reasons to establish the necessary environment for this. Listed below are some of the use cases where predictive analytics delivers value and provides good business support:

- Customer analytics—A combination of demographic, geographic and, if desired, social media data helps define your customers more accurately (360° view). This results in marketing campaign savings; potential and existing customers can be targeted more specifically, and no money needs to be spent on widespread campaigns. Another well-known effect is longer customer retention; it is possible to predict when a customer will churn based on their behavior (customer churn analysis).

- Supply chain risk predictions—When the market rises or falls, resulting ripples can lead to a delayed effect throughout the supply chain. Depending on where your company is located in the supply chain, this can lead to excess stock or out-of-stock situations. With predictive analytics and current market data these ripples can be more accurately predicted. The same can be applied to incoming cash flows and the related risks can be estimated.

- Product profitability forecasting—Product profitability is a result of *revenue* minus *costs*. Factors influencing these two variables include marketing expense, product features, price, lifecycle stage, etc. Predictive analytics estimates the effect of each of these factors on total profitability. It can help predict when a product will go into a late lifecycle stage and when products will sell well or badly.

- Predictive maintenance—With the increase in sensor data processing (IoT), it has become an essential element in today's maintenance approach to identify patterns in a product's manufacturing process. The ability to predict and assess maintenance activities and product/machine failures provides valuable insight for companies; for forecasting, and for minimizing future costs.

As mentioned, there are countless use cases and we recommend evaluating where predictive analytics can help you most.

Predictive analytics use cases

Use cases and success stories from SAP's product SAP Leonardo, can be found at:

https://www.sap.com/documents/2017/01/ 04fa0ad9-a07c-0010-82c7-eda71af511fa.html

We conclude this section with the following recommendations:

- Integrate variable preparation and data quality checks, which are necessary to run models, into your data warehouse or Big Data environment.
- For analytics activities that require data from a Big Data cluster, first evaluate the level of aggregation needed and then decide between basing the model development on the data warehouse or the Big Data cluster.
- Perform error handling in the data warehouse itself. As yet, predictive tools do not deliver many out-of-the-box error handling options (e.g. if not licensed through SAS data integration separately).
- Decide on the exact number of servers you need for a smooth environment execution.
- Use the model management tools to score and evaluate models and to discern which are best and which need to be decommissioned.

3.6 SAP HANA in the cloud

In Section 2.8, we discussed different cloud implementation scenarios: public, private and hybrid cloud. In this section, we discuss the architecture specifics that apply to public cloud and hybrid cloud scenarios. For private cloud, the architecture scenarios we presented in the previous chapters can be applied directly.

From an application layer perspective, the way an SAP HANA BI platform is built generally reflects core ideas of an on-premise architecture. With the approach described at the beginning of this chapter, you continue utilizing data acquisition, data propagation and architected data mart layers. However, the underlying infrastructure which impacts general aspects of the architecture is different, especially in hybrid scenarios. Some topics for consideration are:

- secure user connectivity to the company directory
- secure connection to the company intranet

- patching and upgrading
- data acquisition in the cloud
- applications in the cloud
- remote data access

Amazon Web Services (AWS), Microsoft Azure and SAP Cloud are all possible cloud platforms, and they all offer their own solutions for the challenges listed above. In the upcoming sections we address these challenges, with particular focus on the SAP Cloud Platform (SCP) offerings. SCP can run on SAP's own data centers (at least for productive customer scenarios) located around the world.

3.6.1 User security

Most companies have a central user management (e.g. via Active Directory or LDAP). These central directories are often connected to the company software so that user access rights can be managed centrally. The same can be achieved with cloud platforms. SAP, for example, offers identity provisioning for the integration of Active Directory or LDAP. Prior to this, an Active Directory cloud connector needs to be created. This enables the user to log on centrally in the cloud while user management itself can still be performed from within the company network. In addition, the SAP Cloud has a variety of services for authentication, single sign on, applications access rights, and many more.

3.6.2 Secure company intranet connectivity

In hybrid scenarios, it is necessary to integrate a cloud environment with the company network. This is achieved by opening ports in the company's firewall; but, from a security point of view, is definitely not advisable. The preferred option is to build tunnels which ensure a safe connection via secured protocols such as Transport Layer Security (TLS). This enables access to the cloud servers via the intranet. In addition, data can be securely transferred between the company intranet and the cloud environment. The SAP Cloud Platform solution for this is called *Connectivity* and offers connection options to remote services via http/s, to email providers and, most importantly, to applications in the company network via

Transmission Control Protocol (TCP)/RFC. For SAP applications, RFC connections are used to connect to the company's applications, and a tunnel is used to secure the connection from outside interference.

> **Intranet connectivity**
>
>  Overall, the technical options for secure SAP Cloud connectivity are rather limited (RFC, TCP, HTTP/S, email options). Some of the limitations and prerequisites can be viewed at:
>
> *https://help.sap.com/viewer/cca91383641e40ffbe03bdc78f0 0f681/Cloud/en-US/e54cc8fbbb571014beb5caaf6aa31280.html*

Apart from these connectivity options from the cloud to the company intranet, it is also possible to push data from the company into the SAP cloud. The data is then simply transferred via an outbound https connection to the SAP Cloud Platform.

3.6.3 Patching and upgrading

Most cloud platforms automatically upgrade software and hardware when necessary; this should especially be taken into consideration for PaaS and SaaS scenarios. Although providers inform users of this, the upgrades can still cause issues or breakdowns in your environment. We have seen that miscommunication between a cloud provider and a company regarding these updates can lead to downtime of productive systems, at significant cost. This is a serious issue which has to be taken into account when deciding on a cloud solution. This is especially relevant to SaaS. Upgrades in these scenarios might require code changes in the way implementations were done in the system, or could require a migration to newer versions of objects. SAP's Cloud update strategy is as follows:

For most applications, new releases are delivered quarterly. For some solutions, such as Concur and Ariba, releases are monthly. SAP will inform their customers about upcoming releases several weeks in advance.

> **Handling of upgrades and patches in the cloud**
>
>
> In order to stay ahead of issues resulting from upgrades, we recommend the following:
> - Inform yourself in detail about the upgrade and the cloud provider's patch strategy, and determine if it fits with your company's software release cycle.
>
> - Think carefully about whether to put company-critical applications into the cloud.
> - Define your own service level agreement with the cloud provider regarding availability, upgrades, disaster recovery, etc.
> - Define your own strict governance and process model to ensure no critical information is "lost" during upgrades.
> - For platform-as-a-service products (e.g. SAP HANA in the cloud), define short release cycles, so you can react faster to critical software changes.

3.6.4 Data acquisition in the cloud

Data acquisition in the cloud is not so different to normal data acquisition. There are certain advantages, but also limitations that you need to keep in mind. In the following section, we will look at:

- latency
- cloud connectivity
- scalability
- data ingestion platforms

Data security is also an important consideration; however, we already covered this in Section 3.6.2.

Latency

Latency in a cloud environment can be viewed from different perspectives, especially if the decision on the location of the cloud server is not evaluated carefully. Many cloud providers such as Amazon or Azure offer different cloud server locations around the world in order to decrease latency for end users. This is one type of latency. The other type occurs when loading data. In typical company data centers, the point of data creation and the point of data ingestion are usually physically close together. Data centers are often in the same city.

In contrast, cloud providers do not offer customers many options for data center locations. In a hybrid cloud scenario. The physical distance between a company's data center and the cloud can be much greater, causing high latency. For batch loads, this is not an issue, but for real-time reporting or large scale real-time streaming applications, this impact must be carefully considered. In the case of data streaming, the streaming process might not even work, because data cannot be loaded as fast as it is created.

Data latency

Carefully evaluate the latency issue before you build applications. If you require low latency, we recommend doing a proof of concept first.

Cloud connectivity

Loading data into the cloud has become relatively easy and there are two ways to achieve this: either the data is just pushed into the cloud via https (e.g. the SAP Data Provisioning agent of SDI), or a combination of the SAP Cloud Connector and SAP Connectivity is used to access the on-premise solution via the usual HTTP, ODBC, SAP or RFC connectors from the cloud. The other option involves opening secure tunnels, as described in Section 3.6.2. The choice depends on the security requirements of your company and the confidentiality of the accessed data. SAP Cloud Connector needs to be installed on the on-premise landscape in order for the connectivity to work properly.

Scalability

An advantage of cloud platforms is that they are scalable. At AWS it takes approximately 15 minutes to deploy a new server and content can be easily moved from a small server to a bigger one. SAP servers are also available in the AWS cloud, so you can easily benefit from these solutions. If you use the SCP, you also have access to many SAP applications that Amazon, for example, does not offer out of the box.

Another advantage of using cloud platforms is that you can scale up or down with just a few clicks. There is no need to painstakingly size your solution upfront. Cloud environments therefore help to simplify the building of your architecture. They are also very helpful if you believe that the number of application users will grow, or if you are thinking about building a central platform which will, over time, integrate an increasing number of applications.

Finally, when it comes to IoT scenarios, SAP offers out-of-the-box solutions (e.g. IoT services in the SAP Cloud). However, if you are working with predictive scenarios in the SAP Cloud, you have to consider that SAP Predictive Analytics is not as mature as the SAS or IBM solutions.

Scalability

To scale your applications, and to avoid a long wait for your own on-premise infrastructure to be ready, a cloud platform offers flexibility that you rarely experience in-company. SAP Cloud is a good solution for quick and agile implementations.

Data ingestion platform

A further advantage of a cloud platform is its ability to ingest large amounts of data. When considering Big Data or data lake approaches, cloud platforms offer good options which are often hard to achieve in-company. Once data security concerns have been clarified, you can explore the various enablers for Big Data solutions in the cloud—SAP supplies Hadoop, Hive and Spark-based Big Data platforms in the cloud, and other vendors such as Amazon or IBM also offer Big Data lake solutions.

SAP combines the technologies in the SAP Big Data Services solution. For more information, we recommend the following link: *https://www.sap.com/documents/2017/01/c69fad31-a27c-0010-82c7-eda71af511fa.html*

> **Data ingestion platforms**
>
>  If your company's aim is to build a data lake to evaluate only external data, a cloud platform may well be the best solution. Even if only the analytics results are needed, a cloud platform may still serve as a starting point in order to save money.

3.6.5 Applications in the cloud

One of the biggest drivers for moving to the cloud is the SaaS offers (which we discussed in Section 2.8). A good example of this is Microsoft Office 365, which makes file-sharing very easy and fast. When it comes to SAP applications in the cloud, SAP has a comprehensive portfolio and offering. Furthermore, many consulting companies share their SAP cloud-based assets in the marketplace. SAP provides out-of-the-box software solutions which make it possible to start development immediately, saving you time in bringing your applications to life.

Some of the available solutions include SAP Analytics Cloud, Streaming Analytics and SAP Predictive Analytics. This is one of the biggest benefits of using the SAP Cloud Platform.

3.6.6 Remote data sync

A final feature of the SAP Cloud Platform which we would like to present, is the option for a remote data sync. This functionality is an interesting option in situations where application data is managed centrally and distributed to different continents or countries for user access. This reduces latency for end users and provides an out-of-the-box solution for data distribution to different locations.

> **Remote data sync**
>
>  Remote data sync appears to be a good solution, but be sure not to break any data privacy laws. Data that is shared across borders should be carefully analyzed before using remote data sync.

3.7 SAP HANA mixed scenarios

In real-life projects, you may find that there are factors hindering the implementation of an SAP HANA BI scenario in the exact way we have introduced it. Moreover, you may think about combining multiple components of the various scenarios into one integrated overall architecture. In this section, we will focus on typical, common combinations of components and platforms in today's SAP HANA BI world.

3.7.1 Hybrid SAP BW and SAP HANA native solutions

It is quite common to combine SAP HANA native and SAP BW concepts within a BI architecture. Although SAP BW and SAP HANA native are converging with regard to tools used for modeling and the modeling possibilities, this approach gives you the option to follow an optimal approach; the best of both worlds. On the SAP HANA native side, you benefit from the freedom of designing your data model and working directly with database/SQL operations. On the SAP BW side, you are guided through highly integrated data modeling structures and mature methods to operate your BI solution. SAP has identified a necessity to build a bridge between these two worlds and to unleash the hybrid data modeling potential which comes from this merger (e.g. leveraging calculation functionalities in SAP HANA calculation views and bringing the results directly back to your SAP BW data flow). In Section 3.3 (SAP BW/4HANA), we discussed features that enable you to leverage SAP HANA native features from SAP BW. Some features, such as CompositeProviders, are also available in earlier SAP BW releases. In referencing SAP BW/4HANA in this section, we also factor in SAP BW on HANA.

Let's now look at how both can be equal partners in your SAP HANA BI solution.

Motivation and drivers

We would like to highlight some of the benefits in setting up a mixed scenario with SAP HANA native and SAP BW/4HANA:

- ▶ When migrating applications from any relational database to SAP HANA, logics at a database level can be migrated with little effort (e.g. stored procedures, SQLScript table functions, triggers). An SAP HANA native approach is an obvious solution to use these database components. If you already run an enterprise BI solution on SAP BW and would like to integrate additional database components, then the mixed approach is the way to go.

- ▶ Modeling data in SAP HANA native not only gives the designer more freedom, but also more flexibility to adapt to changing requirements. We have seen multiple client situations, where an SAP HANA native scenario was used for laboratory or prototyping work. This approach supplements the strictly governed structures of SAP BW, which deliver quality-assured reports and KPIs. A typical use case for this concept is the connection of a new data source, on a trial basis, whereby data for a first preview is incorporated into the existing reporting landscape, without passing all quality gates. After the completion of the prototype, a migration into the more strictly governed (SAP BW) world should be considered. In addition, governance principles should still be followed on the SAP HANA native side (see Section 4.2).

- ▶ Although SAP BW/4HANA comes with features for data virtualization (e.g. CompositeProviders), the technical possibilities for working with calculation views on SAP HANA native are richer. Calculating and preparing data without additional persistency can be designed and defined more easily in SAP HANA native. If you would like to combine these results with your SAP BW/4HANA implementation, you should consider a mixed scenario. Note that when it comes to data management and delta handling, SAP BW/4HANA often takes the lead in a mixed scenario. As persistent objects (e.g. ADSOs) provide an automatic view generation, further use of SAP BW data in SAP HANA native objects is simple. However, we recommend taking a close look at the generated objects and thinking about how to use them further (especially because joins are a root cause of performance issues). Please also consider our statements about Data Governance in Section 4.2.

- Front-end tools, especially those outside of SAP, can often deal better with relational database sources than with SAP BW data providers. This is also valid for SAP HANA. In this regard, we have seen implementations leveraging data processing features of SAP BW but utilizing SAP HANA calculation views (built on automatically generated views of SAP BW objects) as the reporting entry point.

- Another point which should be taken into account, is the authorization concept, which is more mature and user-friendly on SAP BW. For this reason, clients usually keep the proven and reliable elements of SAP BW in their SAP HANA BI landscape. Access to data in SAP HANA native objects is then steered via the entry point SAP BW (e.g. by utilizing virtual objects such as CompositeProvider). Therefore, you should consider the front-end tools you are combining with your SAP HANA BI solution. SAP front-end tools can complement the SAP BW authorization concept, whereas other tools are stronger because they have their own data restriction functionality. Consider also whether or not you plan to have a direct SAP HANA native access.

Transactional analytics and SAP S/4HANA Embedded Analytics are also recognized as drivers for a scenario combining SAP HANA native and SAP BW. In BI scenarios which require real-time data, it is beneficial to create (operational) reports directly on the SAP HANA data model from which the data originates, or leverage the delivered SAP S/4HANA Embedded Analytics content. These transactional views of the data can be a source for your enterprise SAP BW solution, requiring a well thought-out link between the involved parties.

Guiding principles

The basic idea of this mixed scenario is to run both approaches on one common platform, and benefit from the overall solution synergy. We therefore recommend you consider and follow the guiding principles defined in the following:

- The fundamental principle of designing a lean and consistent data model has uppermost priority and needs to be considered in its entirety; i.e., keep the overall design of the SAP HANA native and SAP BW/4HANA architecture as simple as possible. Keep the movement and redundancy of data to a minimum.

- Think about the interaction of SAP HANA native and SAP BW/4HANA in your overall architecture. Best practices show that SAP BW/4HANA is often the master technology, which is enriched by SAP HANA native artefacts. Which technological component is the prominent one in your scenario?

- Clearly defined roles and interfaces are important for the success of your mixed scenario. Determine upfront which system serves which purpose in your overall solution. This should cover the data view as well as functional and technical data logics/transformations. This means you need to define exactly which data and logic SAP HANA native and SAP BW/4HANA are in charge of. A look at the connected sources and their business criticality can give you an indication of the importance of the downstream SAP HANA native BI or SAP BW/4HANA solution.

- Do not establish more than one integration layer between SAP HANA native and SAP BW/4HANA. Our project experience shows that building a multi-layered link between the two leads to needless complexity, high maintenance effort, and a lack of transparency when implementing, debugging, or testing the solution. It is mandatory to specify and document common interfaces between SAP HANA native and SAP BW/4HANA.

Technical solutions

Keeping the guiding principles in mind (which are also valid for other mixed scenarios), we will now have a closer look at proven ways to connect SAP HANA native with SAP BW/4HANA, and vice versa. There are three areas in which a link is recommended. Figure 3.11 identifies the three areas in our reference architecture. For simplification, we have excluded SAP BPC embedded from this view.

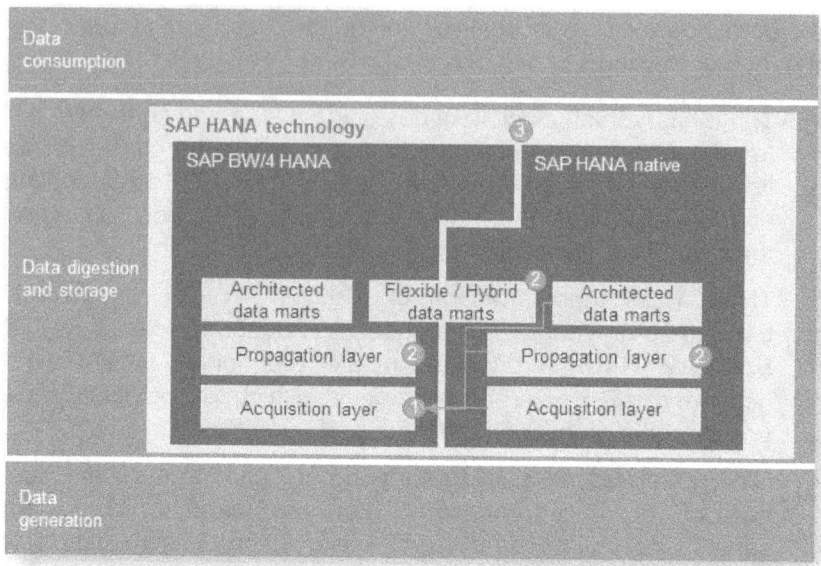

Figure 3.11: Linking areas for SAP HANA native and SAP BW/4HANA

Let's briefly summarize the key characteristics of each linking area:

1. **SAP HANA as source system for SAP BW/4HANA**—In this scenario, calculation views are connected via ODP to SAP BW and are handled as any other source system. Existing implementations (e.g. logics in calculated columns, table functions, etc.) and specific SAP HANA native source system connections can continue to exist without change. This approach can be utilized on any SAP HANA native layer and typically links to the acquisition layer (one-way) on SAP BW/4HANA.

> **SAP HANA native—public and private views**
>
>  For this scenario, we strongly recommend following the concept of private and public views on SAP HANA native. We outlined this in our book *SAP HANA Advanced Modeling* (Chapter 5). By doing so, an interface specification for the ODP source system can easily be established and changes can be handled in a controlled way.

Use of CDS Views as data sources

When using views as a source system for SAP BW/4HANA via ODP, you need to think about how to determine the correct delta. Occasionally, dynamic filters on specific fields of the calculation views are needed. In earlier releases of ODP, we experienced long runtimes when collecting data via ODP from calculation views (compared to the actual execution time of the view itself). So, check upfront that you have the latest updates and notes installed on SAP BW and try to ensure delta/filter push-down to SAP HANA.

2. **Flexible or hybrid data marts**—Both areas have specific advantages in data modeling and processing. To benefit from both, pre-processed data on one side can be made accessible on the other. This scenario is typically implemented on either the propagation layer or the architected data mart layer. Recalling our guiding principles, we again emphasize having only one layer for the link between SAP HANA native and SAP BW/4HANA. On the SAP HANA native side, persisted data from SAP BW/4HANA can be accessed via the automatically generated views (e.g. from an ADSO). At the time of writing this book, virtual SAP BW objects cannot be utilized as a source in SAP HANA native. However, the CompositeProvider is (in addition to the open ODS view) the key object type to link SAP HANA native objects to the SAP BW/4HANA data model.

Limitations of virtual SAP BW data models

When building a mixed scenario on either the propagation layer or architected data mart layer, keep in mind the limitations of CompositeProviders and open ODS views, as discussed in Section 3.3.

3. **Comprehensive reporting solutions**: When we look at the data consumption layer, many front-end tools offer certified interfaces to both SAP HANA native and SAP BW. Based on the origins of a tool (e.g. SQL or MDX), either SAP HANA or SAP BW will be the more beneficial choice. Firstly, products belonging to the SAP product

family show very good integration into SAP BW and can also be leveraged on SAP HANA native. When connecting to SAP BW objects, you need to consider the functionality and performance differences between a direct connection to an SAP BW object (e.g. from SAP Analysis for Office) and via a BEx Query. The latter remains the recommended option because it offers many functionalities that ensure a semantically rich interface to the front-end tool. Technically, you can bring data together from both SAP front-end tools. They are able to deal with more than one data provider; for example, one data provider for SAP BW objects and another for SAP HANA calculation views. For a unified and correct view of your data, report developers have to be careful when working and combining data from different data providers. Alternatively, SAP Universe Designer can be used to combine the two different sources.

> **Query runtimes on SAP BW and SAP HANA native**
>
>  We have experienced big differences in performance and in the way in which SAP front-end tools interact with SAP BW objects, when compared to SAP HANA native objects. Interestingly, there are often cases in which the direct connection to SAP HANA is slow due to inefficient query generation from the front-end tool. However, we have also recognized significant improvements. Be sure to have the latest updates and notes installed and consider the runtime of each data provider when combining them into one report. Furthermore, from a performance perspective, we recommend avoiding direct joins between SAP HANA native and SAP BW objects.

Secondly, front-end tools from the relational database world can often deal better with SAP HANA native than with SAP BW objects. Let us exclude for a moment SAP specifics such as input parameters and custom hierarchies. When going ahead with a non-SAP front-end tool, our experience and recommendation is to run them on the SAP HANA native side and combine these reports with SAP BW data, only in exceptional cases. The question remains, however, whether this theoretically possible case is practicable.

> **Reporting either on SAP BW or SAP HANA native**
>
>  From a best practice perspective, we strongly recommend implementing your reporting either on SAP BW or on SAP HANA native. You should only combine the two at the data consumption layer in exceptional circumstances.

3.7.2 SAP HANA joins Big Data and analytics

Reading the heading for this section, you might think that we are now combining everything we touched on earlier. We are, in fact, focusing on the three core elements that have the greatest influence on today's BI landscape. In recent years, there has been a significant increase in demand for an integration of classic reporting based on in-memory technology with poly-structured mass data analysis and advanced analytics solutions. Market analysis, as well as feedback from our clients, confirm this trend. We have therefore decided to look closer at a typical scenario combining the three areas of SAP HANA, Big Data, and Analytics.

First, let us have a look at the scenario. The core building blocks are illustrated in Figure 3.12, but this is by no means an exhaustive representation. A key differentiator is that the Hadoop data lake environment is used as the central point of entry for all data. The data storage and processing layer acts in the data lake similar to a Corporate Memory in a data warehouse architecture. Ingested data is stored in its raw format in this central location. In order to have semantically rich and reliable information in the Big Data eco system, implementations in this layer need to include data cleansing, metadata tagging, or further data operations Downstream systems are provided via the Hadoop data service and outbound layer, with data according to their needs. Reporting on the Hadoop data lake cluster is also possible here.

In our scenario, we have placed the SAP HANA native (or, in this case, it could also be an SAP BW/4HANA system) as the central reporting platform for classic analysis of structured data. The interface from Hadoop to SAP HANA can only transfer selected, aggregated data. In doing so, costly memory space on SAP HANA is saved. When a report needs more detailed or historical data, a remote access to Hadoop can be added (e.g. by using SAP Vora, SDA). The data already passes quality checks on the Hadoop side, so we do not see a direct need for an acquisition layer on the SAP HANA side (to be verified for each variation of this scenario).

Data scientists often run complex operations on mass data. Therefore, it is beneficial to provide an additional environment for advanced analytics projects. We recommend a physical data replication of required data into the Hadoop analytics environment. Data scientists can then prepare, process, and analyze the data on the Hadoop cluster without interfering with productive processes of the source system.

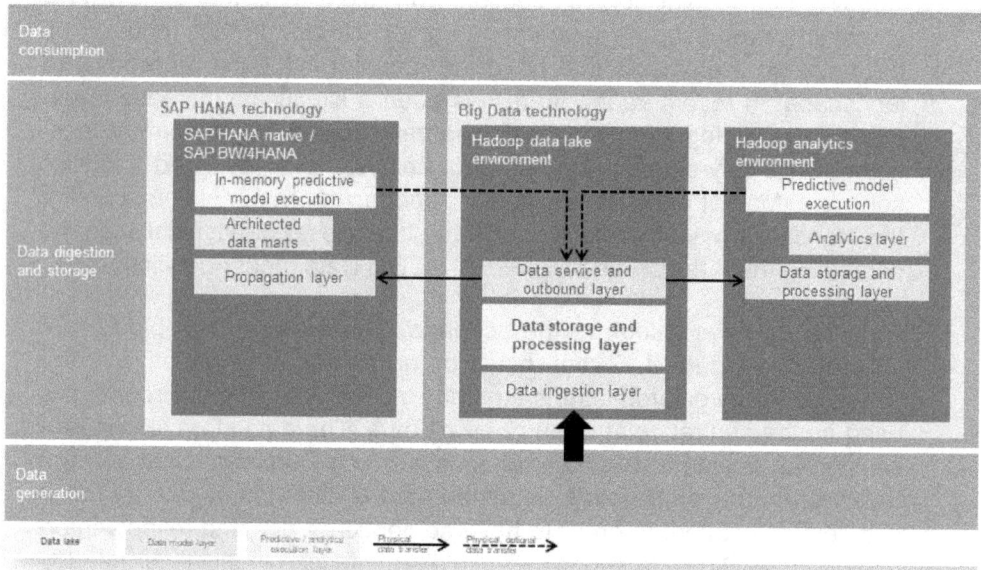

Figure 3.12: Merged SAP HANA, Big Data, and analytics architecture

With the use of Big Data technology, many organizations are about to introduce, or are already implementing, a central data lake. The objective of a data lake is to store all internal and external data in one central place in its original, raw format. In Section 3.4, we had a close look at the Big Data layers, which we also consider to be valid here. The key differentiator in this mixed scenario is that all data runs into the data lake, regardless of type and source. The data lake then serves as a hub, providing and delivering data to any connected system.

> **Organize your data lake**
>
>  You want to avoid your data lake ending up as a data swamp. So, early on in the process, you need to think about methods and tools to enable you to organize and manage your data in the data lake. Data Vault 2.0 (DV), for example, gives you good methodological and modeling guidance in this area, as well as answers for issues such as historization, and auditing. Setting up a proper metadata management can later build on the foundations created with DV. An introduction to DV can be found at: *http://danlinstedt.com/allposts/datavaultcat/a-short-intro-to-datavault-2-0/*.

On the data lake itself, you can execute multi-faceted data analysis. However, if a large number of data scientists need to work concurrently on the Hadoop data lake environment, we usually recommend the installation of an additional cluster environment based on Big Data technology. On this cluster, you should install multiple tools for preparing the data, as well as creating, executing, and validating analytical models. This Hadoop analytics environment should be designated exclusively to data scientists (or similar professions) for complex and advanced analytics scenarios. This environment contains a replication of the pre-processed data from the data lake. Data engineers usually define pipelines to physically transfer data and provide it to the various analytics tools on the cluster. Results of successfully tested analytics models (e.g. PMMLs) can be written back to the actual data lake via its service layer. In doing so, other applications also benefit from the new insights.

Looking at SAP HANA, we see that in this scenario a core data source is the data lake. Following this mixed scenario concept, the data lake also represents the single data source for all SAP HANA-based reporting and analysis solutions. Assuming data already passes some fundamental quality-checks and preprocessing rules in the data lake, there is no need for an acquisition layer; and we suggest directly loading objects into the propagation layer. If (functional or technical) data transformations are needed to meet the specifications of the propagation layer, then the data lake's outbound and service layer should be used before physically transferring the data to SAP HANA. Technical components enabling this data transfer were discussed in detail in Section 3.2.3 and Section 2.4.

The SAP HANA data model stays lean because the propagation layer is now the lowest layer (and all layers on top follow the guiding principles).

> **Interface specification and contract**
>
>  As with all interfaces, we recommend in this scenario that you agree on concrete interface specifications and interface contracts; for example, alignment of responsibilities and owners, agreements regarding data structures, delta specifications, push/pull mechanisms, and exception and error handling. Interface specifications and contracts are beneficial for transparent and smooth platform operations.

SAP HANA also offers analytics capabilities (as discussed in Section 3.5), and we have foreseen the execution of analytical models as the uppermost layer in our SAP HANA environment. As with the Hadoop analytics environment, the results of the successfully executed analytics models on SAP HANA can also be written back to the data lake.

In our mixed scenario, with analytics solutions on both Hadoop and SAP HANA, we emphasize the need to validate each architectural scenario in parallel in order to provide an integrated analytics support on both platforms. In our project experience, we have noticed a more pre-defined focus on internal, structured data when running analytics on SAP HANA. In contrast, analytics on Big Data technologies usually has a wider range of available data. Depending on your analytics plans, and your intended integration scenario (see Section 3.4), we recommend directing the analytics focus to just one platform (often Big Data).

For simplification, we have not highlighted or detailed planning or consolidation interfaces and communication paths (e.g. with BPC embedded). In a non-embedded scenario, classic ETL tools such as SAP Data Services are still popular.

Looking at the data consumption layer, we decided not to open a discussion about the most suitable front-end tools here. However, we would like to emphasize the importance of understanding the various user groups and their specific requirements, from pre-defined, structured reporting to freestyle visual analytics solutions. It is clear a single tool cannot serve all demands in this wide spectrum of end-user requirements.

We strongly recommend first considering the technical and functional capabilities of each front-end tool, including a clear statement on whether this tool will be leveraged on either SAP HANA or Hadoop. Subsequently, the requirements of each user group are matched to the tools. The number of user groups, front-end tools, and assignments of front-end tools to user groups should be kept to a minimum.

SAP has understood the need for an integrated approach bridging SAP HANA and Big Data technology. Below, we outline SAP Cloud Big Data Services and SAP Data Hub, which offer support for Big Data solutions. The SAP Data Hub approach sounds promising when integrating the two platforms.

SAP Cloud Platform Big Data Services

With SAP Cloud Platform Big Data Services, SAP provides a comprehensive Big Data environment including operational services, security, and scalability. A good overview is given at:

https://www.sap.com/documents/2017/01/c69fad31-a27c-0010-82c7-eda71af511fa.html.

Experiences with SAP Big Data Services

Although SAP offers a wide-ranging stack with SAP Big Data services, a lot of software is not included. It is missing a comprehensive metadata and data cataloguing solution. Having once had Alation (Ddata cataloguing solution) in the stack, SAP now plans to have a solution with Jupyter Notebook and the Data Hub. In the meantime, other solutions need to be found. Additionally, HBase and other common database-like products from the Big Data tool suite are not available in the stack. SAP places Vora as its own solution. SAP Vora is not yet available in the SAP Big Data Services platform, but is promised to be delivered (Status August 2018).

SAP Data Hub

SAP Data Hub was released in June 2017. This product addresses key challenges and helps to overcome them when integrating diverse BI components (e.g. linking enterprise data and Big Data, thereby combining complex data scenarios across landscapes). The connection of various data, whether they are stored on-premise or in the cloud, is supported. SAP Data Hub provides tools and services to define, coordinate, operate, and monitor data-driven processes across (BI) environments. For further information, the SAP help pages provide documents and guidelines for the development of data pipelines, the modeling of task workflows, and the administration of the entire environment:

https://help.sap.com/viewer/p/SAP_DATA_HUB

SAP Data Hub trials

In our tests, the SAP Data Hub showed working functionality, and the data pipelines could indeed be modeled graphically. However, often in the nodes themselves, code still has to be added (e.g. in the form of SQL) and the metadata catalogue functionality is still rudimentary. As an outlook, we believe the product has great potential as the latest innovations in version 2.3 show:

https://blogs.saphana.com/2018/10/02/introducing-sap-data-hub-2-3/.

Considerations

This architectural proposal gives you flexibility to manage and work with data on a large scale, and in many ways. Having a data lake as a central corporate memory provides a cost-effective and highly scalable hub that can meet future BI demands e.g. quickly connecting and providing data from new sources to any target. In combining the strengths of the different platforms, your organization benefits from a powerful BI solution. We recommend establishing guidelines and structures at an early implementation stage to keep the end-to-end complexity manageable and understandable and we highly recommend using tools for metadata management, data lineage, and stewardship (see Section 4.2). In addition, you need to determine the characteristics and role of each platform and tool right from the beginning. This includes the interface agreement, data organization rules, and the location of transformation logics within the architecture.

3.7.3 IoT end-to-end scenario

The Internet of Things (IoT) is currently extremely fashionable and is a key pillar of enterprise digitalization. We acknowledge this with our own mixed scenario, focusing on the processing of IoT data. IoT data originates from a wide range of sources; for example, machine sensors, wearable devices, web data from social media posts, log files, geographic information systems (GIS), and media files from mobile devices or drones. To keep our scenario simple (but also transferable to other IoT use cases), we have chosen machine sensors as the input source for our scenario. Based on machine sensors, you can find very popular manufacturing use cases such as machine monitoring or predictive maintenance (e.g. what is the probability that a production machine will break down in the near future, or that a manufactured product will have quality issues?).

> **IoT use case**
>
>
> To describe the architecture and the data flow of our IoT scenario, consider a sensor continuously checking and sending data on the pressure of a water pump. Given a specific threshold, a ticket in the corresponding service system should be generated and an alert sent.

Let us start by defining the core elements and outlining the architecture of our IoT mixed scenario; Figure 3.13 serves as guide.

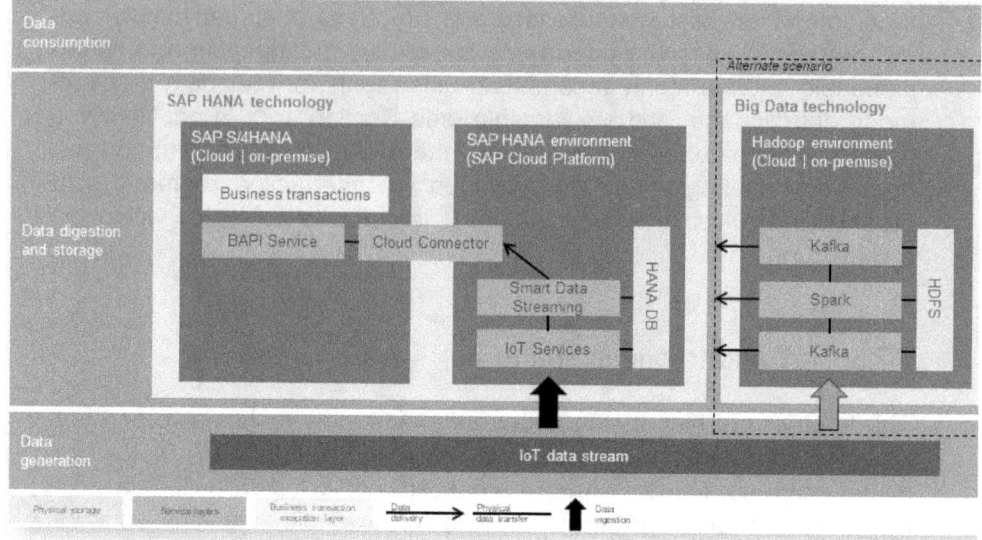

Figure 3.13: Mixed scenario for IoT cases

We'll first focus on the SAP HANA-based part of the IoT-architecture; putting Big Data technology (the part on the right side) aside for a moment. As you can see, the *SAP Cloud Platform (SCP)* is in the center of this mixed scenario. The SAP Cloud (see Section 2.8) provides valuable services and management tools to connect and work with IoT devices and the data they produce.

The data generation layer uses sensors as data sources continuously providing data (e.g. pressure data, as in our water pump example). This is reflected in our architecture as an IoT data stream (as an example of many other IoT sources). Single board computers such as Raspberry PI and Bosch XDK can be used to gather and preprocess sensor data and send it to the SCP (e.g. via the Representational State Transfer Application Programming Interface (REST API) using Hypertext Transfer Protocol (HTTP) post methods). As an alternative to API-based integration, SAP provides the *IoT Connector* (comprising adapter, data processing, and network modules) to bring devices and their data into the SAP Cloud. For the ingestion of IoT data streams, *SAP Cloud Platform IoT Services* are available; the core services are *device management* and *message management*. The benefits of utilizing the SAP Cloud for IoT scenarios include: integrated, existing, out-of-the-box integration tools;

flexibility to scale and adjust your cloud-setup on short notice for new use cases; management of additional data sources, and the ability to provision a user-friendly interface to maintain your individual scenario with minimal effort and directly supervise sensor events.

SAP Cloud Platform—IoT Services

The SAP Cloud Platform Internet of Things Service enables you to develop and operate IoT-related applications in the cloud. Further information about the IoT Service is available at:

https://help.hana.ondemand.com/iot/frameset.htm?ad829c6 60e584c329200022332f04d00.html

Registering and connecting to remote devices to manage the life cycle, from onboarding to decommissioning, is done in device management. In addition, message specifications are determined (device types and message types). As a result, commands can be sent to devices and data can be received. For this, the message management services provides capabilities to collect (e.g. via HTTP, MQTT over TCP API or Web Socket), and forward (e.g. via Web Service using HTTP), or store sensor data (e.g. in the SAP HANA database in our case). Alternatively, the more cost-efficient solution is the event stream, which can also be forwarded to, and stored in, a Hadoop cluster.

Security and authentication

When setting up your IoT landscape, you need to consider security and authentication. Not only do you need a secure connection (e.g. via HTTPS) from the device to your SAP Cloud, authentication tokens are also needed. From our project experience, we recommend not underestimating the infrastructure connection challenges; e.g. sensors with your (company) network or the SAP Cloud. A short proof-of-concept enables you to quickly check the feasibility of your scenario's approach.

>
> **Message Management Service Cockpit**
>
> A service cockpit is available to manage and configure your device settings, device types and message types. It offers support features to obtain authentication tokens. In addition, some basic dashboards are available to monitor and visualize the incoming event streams.

The message management service integrates well with *Smart Data Streaming (SDS)*, or with SAP Cloud Platform Streaming Analytics, and hands over data stream events to it. SDS is designed to analyze, filter and transform event streams in real-time, for exception identification. It helps to monitor incoming data in order to watch for trends, correlations, patterns, and missing data. From this, it can generate alerts and notify applications of specific events so that users can react immediately to the new information. Live updates from the data stream can also be sent to, and viewed by, operational dashboards. In addition, SDS exchanges its data with the SAP HANA database to store events outside the stream.

>
> **SAP Event Stream Processor**
>
> The SAP Event Stream Processor enables the creation of complex event processing applications, and real-time processing and analysis of streaming data. Continuous Computation Language (CCL) is used to analyze the stream data in SDS. It is also used to attach the created adapters to the results of the analysis. See the following document for further information: *https://help.sap.com/doc/download_multimedia_zip-esp_51sp10_esp_ccl_reference_pdf/5.1.10/en-US/esp_ccl_reference.pdf*

In our sample water pump scenario, the event data is forwarded to SAP Data Streaming, which evaluates the continuous stream of incoming pressure values and checks whether they meet a given threshold. Where a value is below or above the thresholds, a notification is sent to a service management system such as ServiceNow, or to an SAP S/4HANA application. In addition, exceptional values are captured in the SAP HANA database. From a cost perspective, storing all sensor values in SAP HANA is not practicable. In real scenarios, cheaper storage solutions such as Hadoop clusters are usually used in cases where you want to store each value ingested by your IoT sources. SDS can pick the values from there for further analysis on SAP HANA. Alternatively, you can analyze and check the threshold events directly in Hadoop and pass exception information to the respective (SAP) downstream system.

SAP IoT Starter Kit

To boost your IoT implementation in an SAP environment, some useful information and code snippets are available at: *https://github.com/SAP/iot-starterkit*

Following our mixed scenario, *SAP Cloud Connector* is used to establish a connection to an SAP S/4HANA system. SAP Cloud Connector easily enables connection to an SAP S/4HANA System using Remote Function Calls (RFCs); communication in the reverse direction is also possible. Therefore, any business function which is available via the Business Application Programming Interface (BAPI) can be called up from the SAP Cloud. In our example, we want to create a service notification in SAP S/4HANA when the water pump pressure sensor reaches a given threshold. One way is to call up the BAPI_SERVICENOTIFICAT_CREATE remote function module. Email notifications can also be triggered.

In addition to this mixed scenario, *Big Data technology* was also included in Figure 3.13. All subsequent explanations are seen as additional to the previously introduced SAP-based architecture. On the Big Data side, stream events can be handled through Kafka. For instance, an event stream is ingested and data is assigned to its associated Kafka topic. Kafka then moves the messages from producers to their consumers. The data stream analysis takes place via Spark Streaming. The handover of processed or selected events to downstream applications can be again done via Kafka.

At any point, a persistence of the events in HDFS is possible. Because Hadoop technology is a cheap way to store data, the full event stream can be stored easily, no matter how large the data volume becomes in the future.

We have talked at length about connecting Big Data with SAP HANA. In Sections 2.7 and 3.4 we discussed the use of connectors built on Spark technology. For the illustrated architecture in Figure 3.13, we include Kafka adapters, which are supported by SDS for input and output transfers. Ingested events on the Hadoop side can therefore be handed over to the SAP Cloud at various layers.

> **Smart Data Streaming and Kafka**
>
>  There are some rather interesting blogs comparing SDS to Kafka, as well as descriptions of how they interact with each other at: *https://blogs.sap.com/2015/12/22/how-does-smarket/* and
>
> *https://blogs.sap.com/2016/05/17/putting-the-kafka-broker-to-work-in-sap-hana-smart-data-streaming/*.
>
> In addition, the SDS Adapter Guide for Kafka adapters is available at: *https://help.sap.com/viewer/34b97bb51d324fe3ace65b3102e453cd/2.0.0 0/en-US/71b4ef6c8b3c40d89eac194b2274a222.html*.

Considerations

From the previous sections, you are now aware that various architectural options are possible and, therefore, decisions need to be made; e.g. to what extent will you consider and leverage Hadoop technology in your IoT scenario? While compiling the components of your future SAP HANA IoT architecture, you should also consider the following questions:

- ▶ Which type of IoT sources do I need to connect? How many stream events will be ingested based on a given time frame, and how often? Which platforms offer the most suitable connectors and programming support for my scenario?

- What SLAs exist for "real" real-time data processing? The tools and mechanisms to ingest and process data vary significantly. Slight delays of a few seconds in the sequential processing steps are acceptable in many practical cases (so, near real-time is often sufficient).
- Do I need to preprocess the data before it enters the SAP Cloud? Are there technical transformations or functional logics to be applied upfront (e.g. via a Raspberry PI?) or can these transformations take place in the SAP Cloud (e.g. in SDS)?
- Think about reusability of logics and rules when it comes to processing and analyzing the data stream. The critical question is where to locate these logics in your overall architecture. We have had a positive experience with SDS in this regard.
- For what purpose will I need the raw/source data in future? Based on this, decide whether there is a need to store each event stream value or just the exceptions. If you want to store all events, think about cheap storage locations such as HDFS. If needed, you can still pick the data for analysis through SDS from there (e.g. by leveraging SDA) and work only with exceptional data values in SAP HANA.
- What applications will act as consumers of the events? How can I best connect to these applications? How many events do they need and how many events are they able to handle in a given period?
- Are there SLAs for providing or processing (exception) events end-to-end?

In general, and for any architectural design decision, think about the overall complexity of your solution. Don't just calculate your costs based on one-time fixed efforts for the setup; also consider the costs for operating and maintaining your solution. SAP has identified that there is a demand for comprehensive, integrated architectures, especially for IoT scenarios and there are now many supporting solutions and tools to help bridge the gaps between the platforms. One of the most important products in this area is SAP Leonardo.

SAP Leonardo

With SAP Leonardo, SAP has introduced a digital innovation approach, which offers development environments, predefined components and solutions for creating IoT-based applications, It provides support for solutions development, using microservices, blockchain, machine learning, and advanced analytics. The SAP Leonardo Foundation provides technical services (e.g. device management, messaging services), data management (e.g. data aggregates or archives), and business services (e.g. application development, use of UIs and APIs). In addition, numerous services and solutions can be built, leveraging the technologies mentioned above to connect people and processes with IoT data. SAP continuously enhances SAP Leonardo, so refer to the following web site for the latest updates: *https://www.sap.com/products/leonardo.html*.

SAP HANA Data Management Suite

The latest terminology within the SAP stack is the SAP HANA Data Management Suite. It bundles a number of known products, including the SAP Data Hub, the SAP Enterprise Architecture designer, formerly known as the SAP Enterprise Architect, SAP HANA itself, and services from SAP HANA (e.g. text search). In addition, it is centered on the SAP Cloud Platform, including SAP Cloud Platform Big Data Services.

3.7.4 Summary

In this section, we have learned about three common mixed BI scenarios for SAP HANA native. To sum up, we would like to outline some general considerations when designing a mixed scenario:

- ▶ Think about the scalability and production-readiness of your mixed scenario. If you include new, immature components into your scenario, you need to include a proper load and performance test in a production-like environment. It is not enough to simply run proof-of-concepts to demonstrate the technical feasibility of an integration scenario when looking at go-live in a productive environment.

- Try to keep the volume of data transferred between the platforms to a minimum. The underlying data model and transfer rules should remain simple. When working with remote connections, keep in mind that there will be some latency in gathering the relevant data. Use filters at the lowest possible layer and work only with data that is absolutely necessary for your reporting scenario.

- Strive for a data model that meets proven standards for each of the technological platforms involved. This helps you, at a technical level, to bring data from various platforms together and to handle structural changes in a well-managed way. Interface specifications and contracts should be obligatory.

- Aim for a single version of truth for your reporting. To achieve this, common semantics need to be established and data values should be harmonized following unified patterns valid for your entire BI environment. As mentioned with the SAP BW/4HANA-SAP HANA native mixed scenario, think about the role of each BI component and the location of technical and functional data transformation logics. Last, but not least, it is worth spending time on the design decision regarding historical data. When different historization concepts are used, the link between the platforms to retrieve meaningful results is different.

- Review and/or update existing Data Governance rules as part of your project (this is discussed further in Chapter 4).

3.8 Migration scenarios

Most existing SAP customers face the problem that in migrating to a new analytics environment, the majority of existing developments, or all of them, have to be rebuilt. This means throwing away ten years of work, or more, building the data warehouse. Most companies do not see it that way, but in our experience, it's a good thing! Most data warehouses were built when there was no governance at all. Many workarounds were implemented which no one understands today, or in even worse cases, some records from old data loads cannot be recreated now due to changes to historical data. Furthermore, over time, many different developers have worked on the data warehouse applications, each with their own style of solution design and programming. If the aim is to keep the old developments, there are ways to migrate from SAP BW to SAP BW/4HANA without losing anything; however, automated approaches are not always straight forward or do not support specific migration cases.

Before going into detail, let's first look at the possible options for migration:

- **Greenfield migration**—everything is built new, without reusing any developments.
- **1:1 migration**—all existing developments are migrated, without any changes to the new environment.
- **Brownfield migration**—some developments are built new and others are migrated 1:1 from the old environment setup.

Each of these scenarios has advantages and disadvantages, and you can choose any one of them, depending on your company's strategy. In our experience, and with a focus on governance, the best approach is often the greenfield approach. However, there are many factors to consider: the financial value for the business, the age and size of the current data warehouse, the complexity of the existing implementation, etc. For each migration scenario, we will look at these factors in detail and make recommendations for the most suitable scenario for specific types of migration; also depending on what you want to migrate.

3.8.1 Greenfield migration

A greenfield migration builds everything new. The goal is to implement the latest business requirements so that the migration provides both business and IT advantages. In most cases, IT profits more than the business—it's a good opportunity to make complex implementations simple again, to reduce maintenance costs and to question the existing status quo. With the greenfield approach, however, the business also has the opportunity to profit from the migration. New features can be implemented which make testing more interesting, thereby adding clear business value as well.

This approach does not require any additional setup for migration. We recommend implementing the new solution separately and consecutively for each business area, instead of choosing a "big bang" approach. Below are some of the learnings from our experience with greenfield migrations to SAP HANA/SAP BW/4HANA:

- **Challenge the business users.** Most of them will say that they want to keep everything as is. However, most reports and analyses are often no longer needed and can be deleted. There are often problems or unnecessary complexities in the old system that need to be resolved. In our experience, redesigning and presenting innovative IT solutions to the business is a practical approach. Demonstrating options and features of a modern BI infrastructure helps to open the mind and create new ideas for renewing existing reporting applications. End users will definitely raise a concern if specific features or content are missing. Therefore, we recommend these users be involved as early as possible, and that you take an active approach to demonstrate and double-check your results with them from the beginning. In addition, try to avoid download functionality in the system, unless requested by a specific application. This only leads to shadow IT solutions.

- **Do not underestimate the effort required for technical issues.** In previous migration projects, we encountered many problems with software bugs, versions, and compatibility conflicts, requiring fixes from SAP. Even with a MaxAttention contract, corrections or solutions can take time and delays of several hours can be critical when following a tight migration plan. Therefore, it is common practice to check your greenfield installation and connectivity before kicking off the actual implementation work, in order to identify possible pitfalls.

- **Be ready to do rework.** It is always hard to explain why rework would be necessary because the solution is brand new, but as the solution progresses, so will your resources' technical experience of the new technology stack. Experience shows that technical issues might require workarounds which can only be fixed at a later time. Intermediate and workaround solutions should be avoided or should at least be directly connected to a mitigation plan in order to resolve the workaround issue at a given point in time.

- **Start implementation early.** At the beginning, you will spend a lot of project time deciding on the best solution, architectural or data modeling approach. It makes sense to first agree on a layered architecture, and naming and general development conventions; but afterwards, move onto proof of concepts instead of getting bogged down in endless discussions that lead to superior concepts that ultimately no one will read or follow.

Below is a list of the biggest advantages of this type of migration:

- With a greenfield migration, you can rectify mistakes, workarounds and governance issues/naming conventions from earlier implementations.
- With the right requirements, management, and good business understanding of IT, new solutions can be managed and proposed. If managed correctly, they result in a higher business value.
- In most cases, performance improvements can be achieved when leveraging the possibilities of the new SAP HANA-based solution options. In our experience, this does not apply to SAP BW queries using the BW Accelerator.
- It is a common mistake to assume that a technical greenfield migration in the IT area alone will result in better and slimmer processes in the data warehouse. However, to achieve this, you also need to standardize and optimize business processes, as well as implement organizational change. This should always be a joint effort; and can also provide financial benefits.

A greenfield migration can also have the following disadvantages:

- The initial cost for the migration can be quite high (e.g. in setting up a new infrastructure).
- Greenfield approaches usually end up in large-scale projects, which rarely finish on time or in budget. Therefore, it's better to split it into smaller projects, with strict requirements and change management.

- If the business does not completely buy in to the project, large amounts of time will be lost in testing. Resources need to be fully available to test the new implementation in order to achieve a high-quality solution.
- For overall satisfaction, you need to ensure a good quality, timely solution, and vendor buy-in. Project participants will become frustrated with the project if it takes too long or requires too much effort, with no clear achievement in the end.

3.8.2   1:1 migration

A 1:1 migration is a technical migration with a direct replacement or adjustment of the old platform's processes. The aim is faster operations and processes on the new environment, but there is often little additional benefit or value for the business. The only possible value is the availability of new software features which the business requires.

SAP offers an automated tool for migrating from SAP BW 7.4/7.5 and the old objects onto an SAP BW/4HANA platform. The tool is called the Transfer Toolbox. The toolbox supports two scenarios:

- in-place conversion on an existing installation, only possible with SAP BW 7.5
- remote conversion with the migration of an existing SAP BW system to a new server, in version 7.0 or higher.

As the tool is currently very new, we recommend doing a remote conversion to avoid problems on productive systems.

For other migrations, such as ABAP code to SAP SDI or SQL code, an automated 1:1 migration is not usually possible. Generated ABAP code cannot be transferred to SQL code or to SAP SDI graphical modeling.

When doing a 1:1 migration, we recommend the following:

- **Automate as much as you can, especially testing**. Business users will be very reluctant to test anything if they do not get any direct value (i.e. they only get a new platform).

- **Use industrialized approaches.** 1:1 migrations can be highly industrialized because many steps, especially on the technical side, are repetitive and similar across migration projects. Industrialized migration offerings help you to save time and money.
- **Test as early as possible.** This principle applies to all projects, but is especially relevant here. In order to keep the project duration short, parallelization should be maximized, meaning that testing should start as soon as possible and be executed in parallel with the migration.

Some of the advantages of a 1:1 migration are as follows:

- Migration time is reduced, in comparison to other alternatives.
- Previously implemented solutions are not lost.
- There is minimum impact on daily business (on end users).

This type of migration has several disadvantages:

- There is often no direct added value for the business.
- You will most likely continue to have defects and bugs.
- In some cases, because of unsupported code lines, manual re-coding is necessary when errors occur in the new system.
- New technology and features are often not leveraged to their full extent (e.g. SAP HANA) because existing objects are just reimplemented instead of optimizing the entire scenario.

In our experience, 1:1 migrations are very risky. The business expects that everything will work as before (which is often not the case) and can get frustrated with the new solution rather quickly. Furthermore, be careful that your 1:1 migration is not purely financially driven. If the project does not deliver the required results, a roll-back is always possible. A 1:1 migration makes sense when you consolidate your IT landscape or move towards a more future-oriented environment.

3.8.3 Brownfield migration

A brownfield migration is a mix of 1:1 and greenfield migration types. A brownfield migration is especially useful when some functionalities of the old environment remain the same, and some are enhanced or rebuilt. In most cases, several core components of the reports and calculations supplied within the data warehouse will stay as they are. This applies in particular to functionalities such as external reporting or internal controlling, but there are many more.

The recommendation here is to first perform a detailed analysis to identify core business components and then identify any missing components (gap identification). Principles from both migration approaches should be combined; for example, industrialization methods of 1:1 migration to save money and, secondly, challenge the business on their requirements, in order to gain the largest business value, as in a greenfield migration approach.

The biggest advantages of a brownfield migration are:

- You can save money on applications, which stay the same.
- The new solutions provide business value.
- New, consolidated guidelines bring the most benefit, even with 1:1 migration elements.

Some of the disadvantages of a brownfield migration are:

- Improvements in 1:1 migration areas may never be discovered because end users do not want to change the way processes are currently organized.
- Top management may not buy in to the project because most elements are migrated 1:1.
- 1:1 migrated elements lack optimization.

Overall, we have not experienced many brownfield migrations because most customers either choose one migration type over the other, but not both together. Some greenfield migrations turn into brownfield migrations, because many existing solutions are reimplemented 1:1. This is due to the fact that most migrations currently stem from an IT initiative, and don't take business processes into consideration.

3.8.4 Comparison of the migration approaches

As seen in the previous sections, all migration approaches have their advantages and disadvantages. Table 3.3 provides a comparison of the migration options against various factors, such as business value and monetary investment. In the table, the evaluation ranges from high to medium to low.

Factor	Greenfield	1:1	Brownfield
Initial investment	High	Low	Medium
Return on investment	High (if requirements are prioritized well)	Low	High (if requirements are handled efficiently)
Added business value	High	Low	Depending on how much redesign is performed, the value can range from low to medium
Project duration	Long	Short	Medium
Best project approach	Agile	Waterfall	Hybrid agile
Tool usage	Agile development tools	Test automation tools, automated development tracking	A combination of both
Effort required for engineering and implementation	High	Low	Medium

Table 3.3: Comparison of migration approaches

3.9 Architecture decision matrix and best practices

A future-oriented architecture for your SAP HANA BI landscape is a major change and requires a detailed analysis of the steps needed to achieve the desired target state. The decision regarding which architecture you need largely depends on the use cases you design and the business benefits you want to achieve. Additionally, some use cases may even require organization and process changes, which you have to be aware of in order to fully leverage the advantages of your planned solution. We cannot foresee all the changes your organization may require, but you can use the two sets of questions shown in the decision matrix in Table 3.4 as a starting point to assist you with the necessary decisions.

Question	Score	Priority (1-5)	Result
SAP HANA vs. SAP BW			
How much of your business reporting has to be conducted in real-time? (5 - very much, 1 - none)			
Historically, how likely is your internal organization to move away from SAP BW to SAP HANA native? (5 - very likely, 1 - not likely)			
Does your business change frequently and/or is there constant technical innovation? (5 - very much, 1 - not at all)			
How strong is the BI governance within your company? (5 - very strong, 1 - non-existent)			
Are the processes within your company locally different (5) or standardized (1)			
How complex is your ETL logic from a historical perspective? (5 - very complex, 1 - not very complex)			
Are your processes similar to the SAP standard processes? (5 - very similar, 1 - very dissimilar)			
How many non-SAP source systems compared to SAP source systems are there in your company? (5 - very many, 1 - not many)			
Do you plan to use SAP HANA as an advanced analytics platform? (5 - Yes, 1 - No)			

SAP HANA BI ARCHITECTURES

Question	Score	Priority (1-5)	Result
Big Data platform vs. SAP standalone data warehouse			
Is your company data-driven (does it work with massive amounts of data), or is your company only using data to stay informed about the current business situation? (5 - data-driven, 1 - data-informed)			
Is your company an innovator or a follower? (5 - mostly innovator, 1 - mostly follower)			
Does your company have access to external data and want to report on it? (5 - yes, to a lot of sources, 1 - not at all)			
Do you need to perform large-scale calculations with large amounts of data, other than, for example, an MRP run? (5—yes, many, 1 - none)			
Does your business work with complex statistical models, requiring large scale calculation powers and/or external data? (5 - Yes, 1 - No)			

Table 3.4: Guide for deciding on architecture elements

These questions help you decide which option is best for your company. To start, answer the first set of questions (SAP HANA versus SAP BW), noting the relevant scores (1-5) for each question in the "Score" column. If you score a 5 for a question in the first part, then for this question the better fitting solution is an SAP HANA native-based data warehouse. If you score a 1, the better solution is an SAP BW-based data warehouse. Scoring mostly between 2 and 4 indicates that a hybrid approach might be best. There are, of course, more definite requirements such as real-time reporting, in which case an SAP HANA native solution is definitely stronger. There are also less definite requirements such as whether governance is well established within your company. SAP HANA enables greater flexibility in the design of the data warehouse solution, which in turn requires greater guidance on how to implement the solutions; as opposed to SAP BW, which delivers its own governance out of the box.

In most cases, you will want to add your own company-specific questions to the table, the answers to which will lead you toward either SAP BW or SAP HANA native. After you have answered all the relevant questions, the next step is to assign a priority to them (1 - low, 5 - high). Then, you multiply "*score* x *priority*" for each question, and note the results in the "Result" column. Next, add all these results up for an overall total. This total then needs to be divided by the sum of the priorities, giving you the weighted average of all questions. To clarify this process, we have added an example below.

Calculating the weighted average in the decision matrix

Table 3.5 shows an example of the decision matrix. The result shown is 1.8 (i.e. 16/9), so an SAP BW-based data warehouse would most likely be the best solution.

Question	Score	Priority	Result (points x priority)
1	5	1	5
2	2	3	6
3…	1	5	5
sum	8	9	16

Table 3.5: average calculation of the table above

Let's now look at the second set of questions in Table 3.4 (Big Data platform versus SAP standalone data warehouse). Scoring 5 points for a question means that the most optimal solution would be a Big Data platform. Scoring 1 point means that a Big Data platform would not provide any additional benefit that could not be realized with an SAP HANA database.

Apply the same reasoning and calculations to the questions relating to Big Data platforms.

We recommend the following general principles to help you make a well-founded decision about your architecture:

- ▶ Be sure to first create a basic requirements specification, carefully weighing up the requirements. The establishment of user stories (based on Scrum methodology), for example, may help a lot.
- ▶ It is important to stick to the overall vision, and question requirements by importance. What may at first seem like a mandatory requirement, could become a discarded optional requirement after the solution has been implemented.
- ▶ When you decide to include a specific architectural element based on certain functional requirements, ensure to use it fully; for example, the architectural element might also be applicable to other functional areas, even though the element was not originally planned to be used in that way.
- ▶ Share your thoughts and make the decision with a broad number of stakeholders. This will, naturally, lead to internal discussions and opposing opinions which may need to be resolved at a higher level; i.e. the program board or even executive board. Be sure to reach a decision supported by all involved parties or which is at least approved within your company. In the end, your architectural picture will be enriched and enhanced to fulfill its intended purpose.
- ▶ Finally, take your time with the initial go/no-go decision. Once it has been made and the implementation has started, there should be no turning back. When challenges in the project occur, you need buy-in from all the stakeholders in order to overcome these challenges. A solid decision foundation helps with the future success of the project.

3.10 Summary

This chapter looked at the elements of an SAP HANA-based BI solution architecture. We started with the general technologies and layers found in a standard SAP BI architecture.

We looked at various architecture variants, including:

- an SAP HANA Native architecture which purely relies on SAP HANA-based elements, the SAP HANA Data Warehousing Foundation and SAP EIM
- an SAP BW/4HANA architecture that is founded on the newly introduced components, like the CompositeProvider or the ADSO
- SAP HANA merged with a Big Data platform architecture scenario as a hybrid architecture
- the advanced analytics scenario, which combines a predictive analytics technology with an SAP HANA-based or an SAP HANA and Big Data-based architecture.
- a cloud scenario where the components of the architecture are partially based in the cloud
- mixed scenarios, which concluded the section on architecture scenarios by showing the possible combinations of the variants above

This chapter also covered the possible options of how to migrate from your current architecture to a new one, such as the 1:1 migration, and greenfield and brownfield migrations.

We concluded with an architecture decision matrix to assist you in deciding on a particular architecture.

4 Organizational principles

This chapter provides an insight into the processes, governance elements, and changes required to implement a working SAP HANA BI architecture; including the concepts of Data Governance, and considerations specific to SAP HANA BI architectures.

4.1 Landscape enablement

"Organization" seems like a simple concept, but in fact, it requires solid planning and a clear roadmap with clear guidelines so you can establish an infrastructure which serves the needs of your SAP HANA BI landscape. Following agile principles, your IT landscape should also be scalable and adjustable, with good flexibility. This presents extra challenges when defining the landscape. What exactly do we mean by "defining your landscape"? First, you may think about infrastructure concepts such as servers, network connectivity and firewalls, or applications to be installed and configured. However, you should also take a holistic view of your future SAP HANA BI landscape, and consider the combination and interplay of technical infrastructure and components, processes, and related applications and data structures. Most importantly, you also need to think about the people working on, and being supported by, that landscape.

When defining the landscape, we encourage you to always remember two things: your **vision** of a modern SAP HANA BI landscape (your aim for the next three to five years) and the **benefits** you would like to get from it. In addition, always update your vision from time to time to keep pace with your current and future requirements. The path, or **roadmap**, towards this vision is not always straightforward. It may require assistance and intermediate steps to help you structure and organize the work into the target state. We recommend conducting a review session after each milestone and looking at the lessons learned. This helps you to adjust and fine-tune future work, and to make go/no-go decisions. Whatever is on your roadmap, think holistically and consider dependencies across the landscape. Following an agile method, each step should provide additional value, especially for end users. Try to separate overall design and implementation work into different stages, so you can see tangible results early on. This can be achieved, for example, by implementing a clearly scoped, small-scale, technical end-to-end pilot. On one hand, this helps to prove your architectural concept and interfaces, and on the other, it gives end users a first visible result (e.g. a simple report with a few selected key figures and characteristics). The first part of your reporting or analytics scenario is then gradually enhanced until it reaches its final version. Before we get to this, we have to detail our vision and roadmap with architectural and design landscape elements, always keeping in mind the processes and end users.

Based on these considerations, you should think about which (SAP HANA) BI **components** best fit your requirements so you can start building the target state of your landscape; the target state is not necessarily the same as the vision, but it should be similar. There are numerous types of components; for example, for data storage, data transfer, analytical calculations, and visualization. This book has so far provided guidance on the available components and how to combine them. In terms of a working environment, sometimes the second-best component is preferable in order to gain integration benefits. Information from the product availability matrix should also be taken into account. In addition, you need to be forward-thinking and consider components that are likely to be enhanced or replaced. As soon as you have your components in place, and a first draft of your architecture designed, you should think about the **interfaces** within your architecture (i.e. inbound and outbound). For each interface, you later define an interface specification and an interface contract. These interface documents help you to align which type of data is transferred, and by which method and mechanism (e.g. push versus pull). Viewing data by function is also possible (e.g. finance, logistics, specific master data). In addition, emergency contacts, in case of failures, are identified.

Following general valid Data Governance guidelines, another key success factor for setting-up and running your SAP HANA BI landscape is the determination of **responsibilities**. Clear accountability needs to be determined and accepted for each part of the interface specification, and for every component and data set. In addition, as with all major IT transformation projects, it is essential to have full support and buy-in from upper management; selling the benefits to management is key to getting their vote. Only with these responsibilities and support can you establish your company's vision of an SAP HANA BI landscape; they also form the backbone your Data Governance (see Section 4.2).

Another aspect of the landscape is its correct **sizing**, and the associated **costs**. You must not forget to look at the total cost of ownership (TCO), including not only repair costs, but also maintenance and operational costs. In addition, you need to take into account the planned production roadmap of the components you plan to use, as well as their scalability for future demands. Sizing tools are available for many BI components, to help figure out the best server/environment size to work on. Furthermore, if you have not done so previously, decide at this point whether you plan to run your architecture on-premise or in the cloud. Sizing, scalability, and pricing might also influence this decision.

As soon as the overview of your SAP HANA BI landscape is ready, start detailing and setting-up the components and their respective interfaces. **Service Level Agreements** (SLAs), which meet the SLAs for the entire SAP HANA BI solution, need to be considered for each component and interface. Your SAP HANA BI solution will not be recognized or accepted within your organization if it does not meet the given SLAs and produce the expected benefits. An effective and future-proof landscape is achieved by selecting the right components and customizing them right from the beginning.

In modern SAP HANA BI environments, we see the need for at least three tiers; development, quality assurance, and production server. Effectiveness, and development and testing quality benefit from independent environments that also enable non-disruptive production operations. *DevOps* approaches can further help to achieve effective and efficient transition to a productive use of your applications. Virtualization of servers, especially for development and quality assurance, is a common cost-saving approach. Don't forget that interfaces and transport paths also need to be defined across the environments.

DevOps

The term "DevOps" is a combination of the words "Development" and "Operations" (as in IT). The objective of the DevOps approach is to achieve a beneficial collaboration through joint processes and tools.

Once you have agreed on your landscape, ordered all the necessary hardware or cloud computing power, obtained the licenses and installed the SAP HANA BI landscape end-to-end, the **operations** and **lifecycle** aspects of the landscape become more important. If you build a landscape inspired by one of the scenarios described in Chapter 3, we strongly recommend having a dedicated operations team which is responsible for keeping your BI solution alive and up-to-date—at both infrastructure and application levels. When new technologies are introduced, you have to ensure that your operations team is sufficiently skilled to handle and integrate these components so you get the most out of new features or technological improvements. Infrastructure and technological understanding are foundations for successful operations. We recommend a lifecycle concept to help guide you with new releases and hotfixes, and any associated components, providing transparency for maintenance and upgrade windows.

The handover of applications to operations also needs a strictly governed process. Typically, the development team performs a small support role after go-live. At the same time, the application is handed over to operations in shadowing and re-shadowing phases. DevOps can help here to design and perform the processes effectively; also taking the entire lifecycle of an application into account until it is decommissioned and attached components are uninstalled.

Last, but not least, we again stress the importance of constantly evaluating the users and processes which will be supported by your SAP HANA BI environment. Involve users from the beginning. Including them in key steps and in planning the setup and future enhancements of your landscape will ensure their buy-in for the overall project.

Your SAP HANA BI landscape will be successfully implemented by following these steps:

- ▶ Create and constantly update your vision of an SAP HANA BI landscape.
- ▶ Select and define the necessary architectural components, always keeping end-user requirements and support for business processes in mind.
- ▶ Define interface specifications and agree on interface contracts, including SLAs.

- ▶ Determine clear responsibilities and roles within your environment.
- ▶ Ensure early integration and smooth handover processes to operations, or follow DevOps concepts.
- ▶ Think about a holistic application lifecycle concept.

4.2 Data Governance

Looking at market drivers (e.g. Industry 4.0, General Data Protection Regulation GDPR, virtual experience economy) and technology trends (e.g. machine learning, Internet of Things, Cloud Computing) behind the SAP HANA BI architectures, it is evident that modern technologies enable organizations to deal with much more data than ever before, under an increasing regulatory framework. The ongoing discussion about organizing data and managing its quality is becoming increasingly important. Data Governance is the practice of combining people, processes, and technology relating to an organization's data and is key for the success of your BI initiative. However, it is not only the benefit of having well-governed data that drives organizations to look into Data Governance, regulatory requirements can also force them to invest in this area. The key objective should therefore always be to increase business efficiency through increased data quality and easy search and data retrieval mechanisms. Typical examples here are: a reduction of data duplications (finding the version of truth more easily), an increase of data accuracy and completeness, and the advantage of new Google-like search mechanisms to quickly identify the data needed to support the decision you have to take.

Definition of Data Governance

A comprehensive guide to Data Governance, published by The Data Governance Institute, serves as a good starting point. It is available at:

http://www.datagovernance.com/wp-content/uploads/2014/11/dgi_framework.pdf

To support your SAP HANA BI initiative, we strongly recommend initiating a Data Governance program; bring all relevant stakeholders together and agree on rules, responsibilities and guidelines for all data in your BI/analytics scenario. Business users generate and work with the data, so they are the ones who usually own and drive Data Governance. IT has the role of providing frameworks and software supporting Data Governance. This can be software for master data, data quality, or data lifecycle management. Within your Data Governance team, make sure roles and responsibilities are clearly defined and established. From an organizational perspective, you need to hold regular meetings for updates on the visions and goals of your Data Governance approach; otherwise, neither Data Governance nor your SAP HANA BI project will deliver to your company's high expectations.

Data Governance dimensions

Let's now focus on the various dimensions you have to consider regarding Data Governance:

- **Data Lineage** is the process of tracing and visualizing the path that data takes through your system, from its origin to the end target; for example, you want to identify which field/s, and in which source system/s, a specific characteristic in your report comes from. The metadata of each component in your SAP HANA BI architecture needs to be compiled at a central location, and the interdependencies and connections documented. To visualize the dependencies in a graphical presentation, we recommend SAP Information Steward because it interacts well with SAP-based sources (e.g. SAP S/4HANA), SAP ETL tools (e.g. SAP BO Data Services), and also with your SAP HANA or SAP BW systems and its connected front-end tools based on SAP Business Objects. For SAP-focused environments, SAP Information Steward is a good choice.

- **Data Quality** focuses on accuracy and completeness of data. Uniqueness of the data also plays an important role. In today's data-driven world, data is often redundant or ambiguous way (e.g. in Big Data or Data Science scenarios where fuzziness in results is accepted). However, ensuring the quality of data, especially in traditional, classic reports is a must. We have seen that great effort is made in analytics to identify and correct faulty data (as always, this should be done at the source). SAP BW supports data quality checks and its well-known standard functionalities, such as checking master data against transactional data or the error data store object. At the SAP HANA level, Smart Data Quality (SDQ) provides good functionalities in this regard (e.g. for cleaning address information). It is generally used with Smart Data Integration (SDI) as part of the SAP EIM solution. SAP Information Steward or SAP Data Services both offer strong capabilities to improve and ensure data quality. Independently of the tools supporting your Data Quality endeavors, we strongly recommend implementing a structured process to supervise and measure data quality by identifying, analyzing, and correcting faulty data records. Data quality scorecards help you to visualize your progress in this area. A self-reliant but highly important area of data quality is master data quality. In each case, it is important to determine the lead system for master data, and manage its quality.

SAP Master Data Governance

SAP provides a sophisticated product for Master Data Governance (MDG), also delivering SAP HANA-optimized business content objects. Further information can be found at: *https://www.sap.com/products/master-data-governance.html*.

- **Metadata management** is another important Data Governance discipline; it unites and harmonizes the system's metadata. It is important to consistently provide a clear understanding of an organization's data. Metadata management can be broken down into various levels, such as:
    - **data visibility**, which gives transparency of data owners, supported processes, and sources. It enables you to define accountability for the expected result delivered from a specific set of data, and helps to support reusability of data.
    - a **common understanding** of the data, via an agreed business vocabulary across your organization's different departments.

▶ an **audit** trail, which is often required, especially when your BI solution needs to fulfill regulatory requirements. Metadata management processes, such as tracking load dates and times, consistent creation of error messages, and tracking changes in the data ensure traceability.

SAP BW integrates well with SAP sources and is good at reading and consuming their metadata (e.g. when leveraging standard extractors or interfaces such as BADI to get full field information). However, this metadata is often limited to a business/functional level. The same applies to SAP HANA native scenarios. Strong and semantically rich metadata management support is provided by external tools such as SAP Information Steward in combination with specific metadata integrators or additional tools such as SAP Power Designer. Looking at the Big Data world, with Apache Atlas, we find a metadata and Data Governance framework which offers similar support for data classification, audit trails, and data lineage.

▶ **Data security** has different forms and levels. We view data security as the situation of allowing only authorized data access and data operations. This raises typical questions such as—who is allowed to see or access which data? A widely used approach here is to group users by organizational specifications. What data operations are allowed for a specific user? Here, a user-group classification is helpful (e.g. classifying users as standard report users or expert users). A combination of the necessary data access and the data operations of each user group results in a matrix authorization concept. SAP HANA native and SAP BW/4HANA both provide sufficient functionalities for implementing a solid authorization concept, but we find that SAP BW's solution is more mature and easier to handle. In addition to the authorization concept, data security contains all measures and mechanisms to avoid unauthorized access. Encrypted communication channels and the encryption of data are included in this area, as well as anonymization of data (e.g. personalization). For these areas, individual solutions according to the given requirements in your SAP BI environment have to be developed. From a governance perspective, the tools and products on the Big Data platform have taken great steps forward. For instance, the

Apache Ranger product helps you to manage and monitor data security across your platform.

▶ **Business processes** also need to be considered in a holistic Data Governance solution. Looking at your organization, processes and structures need to be adjusted and aligned in order to efficiently use the new options and features of a modern SAP HANA BI solution, and to achieve the best results. This touches not only on streamlining traditional reporting processes but also introducing new ways of working (e.g. data science methods) to enrich or gain new insights. The impact and necessary adjustments of Business Processes is even more important when your new BI landscape is composed of various technological platforms. A good example is when your revenue analysis is enriched by sentiment analysis conducted on your products on social media posts. Sentiment analysis uses elements of natural language processing, computational linguistics and machine learning to determine or characterize the sentiment of content of a text unit. Your managers not only look at one-dimensional sales figures but can also check online feedback and market news, and decide on effective campaigns to increase sales.

It becomes even more important to define, implement and continuously follow Data Governance guidelines when there is more than one system or platform technology in your overall BI scenario. In the course of this book, we have had a close look at SAP HANA BI architectural scenarios, many of which incorporate platforms or tools that are not directly part of the SAP HANA family (e.g. Big Data). In these scenarios, we highly recommend thinking about proper Data Governance guidelines in a comprehensive approach. We encourage you to think about end-to-end-scenarios when defining your Data Governance rules. If you fail to bring all the platform/technology stakeholders to the table, to clarify and agree on ownership, responsibilities, master data systems and data quality rules, then the implementation and operation of your BI system will not be effective. Most likely, you will not achieve a trusted and integrated BI system.

Our experience shows that, especially in BI environments, you cannot achieve a trusted Data Governance without the full buy-in, support, and ownership of the business and their IT representatives. Therefore, think about establishing a Data Governance committee which closely follows all applications and changes during the entire lifecycle; from initial demand and conceptualization through to implementation, testing, go-live and decommissioning.

When we look at possible tool support for our Data Governance tasks, we find only a limited list of tools which can handle multiple independent technology stacks; e.g. SAP HANA combined with Big Data. Often, a specific tool has its origin in a specific technology and has been further developed or enriched by interfaces to other platforms. In this way, the functionality for the secondary technology is limited and often reduced to just reading operations. A good example is data lineage. There are tools such as SAP Information Steward that can also retrieve metadata information from Big Data environments. Other tools with a rich set of data lineage functionalities are Informatica's Enterprise Information Catalogue and IBM Infosphere. The creation of a central, global metadata repository is recommended and is the preferred solution over distributed local repositories for integration scenarios.

Another challenge with SAP HANA BI systems that work closely with other platforms are data quality gates. When exchanging data between the platforms, additional quality checks should be implemented at the receiving end. In an ideal world, the system processing the data ensures its quality. However, as project experience has shown, each platform has its own standards and technical requirements for working on incoming data. We see the need for a data quality gate in the first layer of the receiving system.

Last, but not least, we would like to highlight data security and authorization questions in an SAP HANA BI architecture which also takes other platforms into account. A Big Data platform, for example, works with different techniques and solutions when it comes to authorizations. Looking at data, the same basic questions arise—who is allowed to see what data? and what are they allowed to do with this data? Only the technical realization is different. For an SAP HANA BI solution which combines various technological platforms (e.g. Big Data), it is not possible to have only one combined technical solution to maintain and check authorization rights. In contrast, authentication can be easily centralized by using central directories (e.g. Active Directory, LDAP). However, before you spend too much time thinking about this issue, start with a view of your user groups. Most likely, the users working directly on SAP HANA are different to those working on the Big Data platform, which is often used by data scientists. For the small group of users who need access to both, you either export their user privileges to SAP HANA (assuming they are already SAP users) and think about a smart transformation of the CSV file to import it into the security framework of the Big Data platform (e.g. Ranger).

Unfortunately, when it comes to Data Governance, these are not the only challenges with mixed SAP HANA BI architectures. However, with a central metadata repository, a sound data lineage mechanism, and proper (not necessarily fully-integrated) data security and authorization concepts, you will have made a good start on your Data Governance journey.

4.3 Development environment

Development within a multi-layer architecture has always been difficult because many dependencies and objects cannot be changed without affecting other objects. This does not really change with newer BI architecture you might build, but there are specifics to consider with the new toolsets.

In this section, we will take a closer look at the following areas:

- parallel development within the entire architecture
- debugging
- end-to-end testing
- transport/deployment of developments

4.3.1 Parallel development

Parallel development with independent systems is usually simple. However, when you have several systems depending on each other with data feeds between them, special governance is required in order to guarantee they work in parallel (see Figure 4.1).

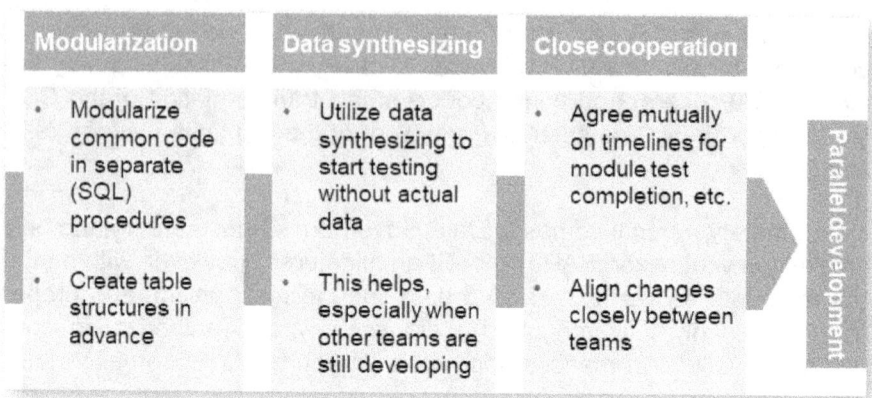

Figure 4.1: Key considerations for parallel development

Parallel development in an analytics environment is often only possible when data flows are completely separate; however, speed and agility are receiving more and more focus, so these key points help in improving agility and development separation.

As Figure 4.1 shows, one of the most important aspects is **modularization**. Modularization can be easily accomplished when writing code (e.g. in Java) but is more difficult with graphical modeling tools. The advantage of scripted code is that functions that are often used can be put into a container and reused by other functions. However, in graphical modeling this is not so easily achieved. Informatica, for example, offers the options of reusable lookups or maplets, which represent a chain of reusable commands. In SAP BW, transformations themselves are not reusable. In SAP SDI, a data flow must have a start and end table. The only way to really reuse transformation logic is through SQL procedures (in both SAP BW and SDI) or with ABAP code (in SAP BW only). There is, however, a slight difference when it comes to SAP HANA (CDS) views. If, at first, a view is only defined with its output structure, further work can potentially continue over top of this. Refer also to the concept of public and private views, which we explained in detail in our previous book **SAP HANA Advanced Modeling**. A modularization in the classic sense is not possible; i.e. where individual functions are put into one function with only some input parameters.

Modularization is achievable in a Big Data environment connected with SAP HANA, because the environments are often code-based. Passing data to, or loading data from, the Big Data environment via SAP Vora, for example, is easily modularized. In this case, the interface for SAP HANA is only the remote table definition, containing a set of fields and their datatypes.

Table 4.1 shows typical modularization options:

Modeling tool	Easy modularization possibilities
SAP Smart Data Integration	SQL procedures
SAP HANA Views	SQL procedures, SAP HANA views (beware limitations)
SAP BW Transformations	SQL procedures (partial, requires use of physical tables), ABAP functions/classes
SAP Vora	Virtual tables as interfaces
SAP Predictive Analytics	SQL procedures, R code

Table 4.1: Modularization with SAP's modeling toolset

Recommendations for modularization:

- ▶ Set up the table structures first (inbound and outbound). Table structures may change and then need to be adjusted in the dependent data flows, but this allows for development of dependent items in parallel.
- ▶ Only use SQL-coded procedures if the functionality is reused often, or if you are using SQL code. SQL coding requires experience but graphical modeling maintenance is more accessible because it is easy to learn and read.
- ▶ Only modularize functionalities that will be reused.

The second major aspect of parallel development is **data synthesizing**. Data synthesizing is typically used for module testing in offshore projects or if you do not have any data available for testing. The second part is especially true if you do upstream developments without the downstream development having been finished. In our project experience, we often see issues arise when using synthetic data only. Their coverage is often not sufficient for comprehensive testing, but simple errors can be resolved. Consider this as a supportive step to enable your teams to continue their developments, and first execute some fundamental testing procedures.

Data synthesizing

The steps for data synthesizing are comparable to test-driven development:

1. Analyze the data processing steps and transformation rules.
2. Define the possible test cases for each rule (e.g., null values being passed, min and max values, and strings instead of integers).
3. Put these cases together (e.g. into one spread sheet).
4. Design a dataset to cover each of these cases.
5. Insert the dataset into the source table.
6. Run your workflow and resolve any issues.

The last point regarding parallel development is probably the most important and the most difficult—**coordination**.

In our experience, when the outputs of several teams are dependent on each other, a strict enforcement of governance is necessary. This means that every structural change needs to be coordinated between teams, thereby requiring additional effort.

> **Coordination of structural changes**
>
>
> Imagine that a field in the main customer table is renamed from "customer status" to "customer activity". This table comes from the Hadoop environment via an SAP Vora remote table. It is loaded into the data acquisition layer, into an ADSO in SAP BW or a table in SAP HANA. This change has the following implications:
>
> ▶ The remote table needs to be refreshed and renamed.
> ▶ Objects associated with this field will no longer work or will be invalidated.
> ▶ Existing tables need to be adjusted.
> ▶ Data flows need the field to be renamed.
> ▶ Modularized functionality is not directly impacted; calls of modularized functions by the data flow might need adjustment

This process seems easy, but when performing such a change, each team member must be aware to perform the change smoothly.

In our experience, this can only be achieved if all team members, and especially team leaders, actively follow this process, and if changes are centrally communicated and tracked.

4.3.2 Debugging

Debugging with SAP BW/4HANA, SAP HANA and SDI has become much more difficult than it used to be in a traditional SAP BW-only world. When implementing an SQL routine in an SAP BW/4HANA or SAP BW on HANA transformation, developers can use the SAP HANA SQL procedure from SAP BW in order to debug the procedure. First, a breakpoint should be set in the corresponding SAP HANA SQL procedure to ensure line-by-line debugging can be performed. SAP SDI offers the option to debug data after each node via the *Just-in-time (JIT)* functionality. This can be enabled for each node, and results can be checked.

In SAP HANA views, debugging via SQL works more easily because break points can be set, and SAP HANA offers a separate debugging functionality for SQL. Additionally, CDS views can now also be debugged, even if designed graphically, but only for the generated SQL per node.

Table 4.2 summarizes the debugging options per modeling tool.

Modeling technology	Debugging option
SAP Smart Data Integration	Only via intermediate tables created physically in SAP HANA
SAP HANA Views	SQL Views via SQL (ABAP Development Tools—ADT) debugger; CDS views with an SQL analysis per node, and SAP HANA calculation views only via developer design
SAP BW transformations	ABAP Debugger tools, for AMDP—AMDP Debugger
SAP Data Hub	Via Kubernetes or in the pipeline modeler
SAP Predictive Analytics	Only at log file level
SAP HANA SQL Procedures	ADT debugger in SAP HANA

Table 4.2: Debugging options in a mixed environment

4.3.3 End-to-end testing

End-to-end testing in a hybrid environment has its challenges because data flows need to be tested across system borders. Therefore, particular focus should be on the interface between one system and the other.

We recommend the following measures to achieve solid end-to-end testing, even if the data processing logic between systems is kept to a minimum:

- ▶ Implement minimum logic, or no logic at all, when transferring data between two systems. This reduces test effort and avoids the problem of data reconciliation between systems, which often requires the analysis of system log files if records are missing. The analysis of logfiles is necessary in all cases when data is not transferred to the target system. However, if there is logic between systems, you can have an additional error source because the root cause could be an issue in the logic.

- Use test automation tools as much as possible. With the new DevOps and test automation initiatives, there are tools that not only support java coding in the cloud, but also ETL software; for example, you can use DBFit to test based on database tables, or Informatica offers the Data Validation option to automate ETL tests.

- Define standard test cases covering all known cases and problems. Regression testing then becomes easier.

- Tests on data throughput between systems and load performance evaluations may be more interesting than single platform environments. This can have an immediate impact on user satisfaction. Running tests can be as easy as loading a large amount of data from one system to another, then checking query performance on the source system and the insertion time on the target system. To test network performance, there are several tools on UNIX/Linux (e.g. through the iperf command).

- Real-time applications may be difficult to test with the latest data. In order to evaluate the correct implementation, relevant snapshots should be taken. To test the latency between the source system and the target system, a separate test is required to measure the time needed for retrieving the required data.

- Standard testing guidelines (e.g. modularization of tests, test completeness) also apply for new architectural design, as discussed throughout this book.

4.3.4 Transport/deployment of development objects

In a combined Big Data/SAP HANA eco system, there are obstacles in the deployment of development objects, especially when everything needs to be coordinated and synchronized so that no deployments fail due to missing objects in the source or target environment. Even in a single SAP BW system, line deployment often fails due to interdependency between objects. Naturally, the problem becomes worse when more systems are involved.

The key to mitigating the situation is modularization, but also close tracking and cooperation between teams.

4.4 Data security and authorizations

When discussing the introduction of Big Data environments with our clients, some of the most critical concerns raised at the beginning were regarding data security. Previously, most Big Data platforms had minimal security concepts and authorizations were hard to manage. This has changed over the years and technology, as well as underlying concepts, have evolved. However, in a hybrid architecture, or in a hybrid cloud architecture, this issue of security and authorization is still difficult to handle. In this section, we will focus on security and authorizations from a user-access and cross-platform integration perspective. (We will not cover infrastructure-level security such as network level security, server-to-server communication protocols, firewall software or other measures that ensure application and intracompany security.)

First, let's look at the different usage scenarios in hybrid Big Data and SAP HANA/SAP BW systems which lead to a more differentiated view of security, privacy and authorizations.

From our perspective, when it comes to data consumption, there are four internal user groups (e.g. using reports or data analytics tools). This list is not exhaustive and we exclude developers, testers, and external users, who may also have access to the Big Data platform.

- **Managers** are often especially interested in dashboards and regular KPI reporting. These reports usually only rely on structured data and require a data warehouse structure in order to deliver these KPIs in a standardized and reliable way.

- **Operational and standard business users** need more detailed reporting, often in tabular format. Analyses can go down to a more granular level of single transactions (i.e. operational reporting). Some of these users access the operational system directly and are even allowed to change records directly. Depending on the architecture you choose, this user group may require access to more than one system.

- **Power users** use drill-down functionality in reports, explore data, and formulate requirements for new reports. This is the first user group that may require access to the Big Data platform and SAP systems.
- **Data scientists** explore new and "unchartered" data to find previously unknown connections and relations in the data. This helps the company to understand their business better and results in further reporting requirements. These users mostly work in the Big Data environment, but may also require access to a more structured data warehouse.

Each of these user groups may have select users, with specific business tasks, who require access only to the Big Data platform, (e.g. to analyze and react on social media posts). For subsequent explanations, we would like to keep it simple and focus on the groups listed above.

Looking at these user groups, two things immediately become clear:

1. Most users are in the operational and standard business user group.
2. In a typical hybrid SAP HANA-Big Data scenario, only power users and data scientists require access to the Big Data platform and the data warehouse. Depending on your data storage strategy, data scientists will likely only access the Big Data environment if, for example, all data warehouse data is also transferred to the Big Data environment.

Now let us look at authorizations:

- When working in an SAP-based ERP, SAP BW or SAP HANA native solution (Scenario 1), authorizations are generally easy to handle across platforms. SAP BW and SAP HANA both require slightly different concepts, which we will take a closer look at later in this chapter.
- The integration of security and authorization objects between SAP HANA/SAP BW and a Big Data platform (Scenario 2) is much more difficult to handle. So far, there are no standard solutions in the market for this specific area. We will look at the requirements for this and suggest solutions later in this chapter.

- ▶ The Cloud (Scenario 3) also has its own challenges. Users access data over the internet, which potentially allows for middleman attacks and simple entries via password hacks. There is no straightforward solution for this, but we will have a look at some initial measures.

- ▶ Finally, there is the integration between the front-end tool and the backend platforms (Scenario 4), but we will not cover this here. They both usually work through SQL/MDX or some other standard access technology. Most frontends allow for further restrictions regarding user access, but they should not handle security at record or table level. We recommend looking at the security options of your chosen front-end tool for making your environment more secure.

Looking at user groups and platform integration, we can now make some further observations:

1. It is rare to have a situation where users need parallel access to both an SAP environment and to Big Data. Only data scientists and BI power users should be considered for this combined access.
2. The most difficult integration of authorizations across platforms is when the Big Data platform is combined with SAP technologies, because the vendor and technology stack change completely.
3. The cloud requires its own set of rules and delivers further complexity regarding security and authorizations. Although the SAP Cloud offers an integration service with your company backend, there is still the issue of restricting access for outside users, for example.
4. Finally, managers and operational/standard business users will most probably only access data originating from internal SAP-based systems such as SAP S/4HANA, thereby making access management easier; the integration between SAP tools is much easier to manage in comparison to other technologies or platforms (e.g. Big Data).

Figure 4.2 shows the relationship between these considerations and serves as a guide for the rest of this section. We will discuss each of the previously-mentioned integrations separately. Cloud integration (Scenario 3) spans all of the areas shown in Figure 4.1 and will also be treated as a separate topic at the end of this section. The scenarios outlined in this graphic refer to the integration scenarios described earlier and do not necessarily correspond directly to user reporting requirements. As you can see in Figure 4.2, power users and data scientists are the user groups requiring comprehensive access for more detailed data analysis on the Big Data platform. This does not take into account using the Big Data platform for further standard reporting which is not covered with your data warehouse, or doing all reporting in the Big Data environment (Big Data Warehouse).

	SAP S/4HANA	SAP BW/4HANA	SAP HANA native	Big data platform
Executives / Managers	Scenario 1.1 X (operational managers)	X* (standard reporting)	X* (standard reporting)	Scenario 1.2
Standard users	X (operational users)	Scenario 1.3 X* (standard reporting)	X* (standard reporting)	
Power users	X** (operational reporting)	X* (report analysis)	Scenario 2 X (report analysis)	X** (might require access)
Data scientists			X** (might require access)	X (finding new data connections)

*Usually only need access to either SAP HANA or SAP BW data
**Dependent on the data duplication across environments and the information needed

Figure 4.2: Security and authorization concepts

Let us now take a closer look at each scenario.

4.4.1 General technical solution approaches

In the SAP world, there are several technical approaches that help achieve a solid foundation for authorizations. First, SAP offers the SAP identity manager for centrally maintaining roles and users across SAP systems. However, this does not include Big Data authorization management, which requires an additional solution.

A second software used in Big Data authorizations can be Apache Ranger, for example, which provides a central solution for governing and restricting access across your Big Data platform. Ranger delivers the possibility to manage users, roles, and security at a file level, or at a table and column level. This works well in a Hortonworks environment. There are other vendors and software such as Apache Sentry, and distributions such as Cloudera and MapR, which offer their own solutions for role and user management.

> **Apache Ranger**
>
>  For further information on the Apache Ranger software, we recommend the following website:
>
> https://ranger.apache.org/

Another concept which has established itself in the area of user management, is Lightweight Directory Access Protocol (LDAP). It works with all the previously-mentioned platforms and enables a company-wide central user management for names, email addresses and other information, making user creation on a new platform much easier. We strongly recommend using this protocol on all your platforms.

There are further authentication protocols such as Kerberos (LDAP also delivers this possibility, but Kerberos is more secure), Transport Layer Security (TSL), and many more. However, we will not go into detail on these.

4.4.2 SAP S/4HANA and SAP BW/4HANA integration

SAP S/4HANA and SAP BW/4HANA both rely on ABAP-based authorizations, making handling a little easier than when using different technologies. Many companies already centrally maintain their roles and users for SAP BW and SAP ERP in the SAP identity manager. This works for SAP S/4HANA and SAP BW/4HANA in the same way. In contrast, SAP BW usually combines data from different areas in the company, thereby sometimes rendering operational authorizations concepts ineffective, or even obsolete. Until now, authorizations for operational reporting have had to be defined separately. Today, SAP Fiori is a recommended tool for operational reporting, with SAP S/4HANA as the basis. In this scenario, SAP S/4HANA authorization concepts and SAP HANA-based authorization concepts can be used (e.g. application authorizations, analytic privileges and roles).

> **SAP HANA authorization concepts**
>
>  For further information on SAP HANA authorizations and concepts, refer to the SAP HANA security guide:
>
> *https://help.sap.com/doc/eec734dbb0fd1014a61590fcb541 1390/1.0.12/en-US/SAP_HANA_Security_Guide_en.pdf*

With SAP BW/4HANA, completely new authorizations and roles have to be defined; this differs to the old SAP BW world with InfoCubes, standard DSOs and MultiProviders. However, as used in previous SAP BW versions, the concept of analysis authorizations and the usual roles are continued. This allows for a restriction on certain InfoProviders and queries, as well as at data record level.

4.4.3 Hybrid SAP data warehouse and SAP S/4HANA scenario

When it comes to security and authorizations, the good thing about a hybrid SAP BW/4HANA and SAP HANA native architecture, in combination with SAP S/4HANA, is that there is not much difference to a scenario with SAP BW/4HANA and SAP S/4HANA. As discussed previously, SAP BW/4HANA enables you to publish SAP BW objects as SAP HANA views with the corresponding access rights, directly translated to SAP HANA objects. However, be aware that these rights will only apply to SAP BW objects and any SAP HANA views built on top. Any other SAP HANA view you create separately (not on top) will not use these restrictions, even if they are constructed on the same InfoObjects. Here, we strongly recommend evaluating beforehand your hybrid scenario's exact use case and whether it requires additional authorizations on the SAP HANA native side. You also need to think about what the leading platform should be from an authorizations point of view. Where further authorizations or details about implementing your specific security requirements are needed, we recommend reading the SAP HANA security guide referred to previously.

4.4.4 SAP S/4HANA and SAP HANA native

In this particular architecture, two separate authorization concepts are required. First, you need restrictions regarding the kinds of transactions users are allowed to perform and which input fields they may alter. In addition, SAP Fiori authorizations are necessary in order to work on and analyze the SAP S/4HANA data.

When it comes to SAP HANA data authorizations to restrict user analysis to row level, analytic privileges are once again part of the picture. If you run an SAP HANA native data warehouse, there is a chance that these privileges might be replicated and reused in your analytical world (with minor adjustments for different tables and labeling of views).

SQL-based privileges can potentially use the same table to define user access rights in your SAP HANA native data warehouse and your SAP S/4HANA system.

> **SQL-based privileges**
>
>  If you invest in this scenario, we strongly recommend gathering more information on SQL-based privileges.
>
> See:
>
> https://help.sap.com/viewer/fc5ace7a367c434190a8047881f92ed8/2.0.00/en-US/40e68279bed0498aa10bc8bac6ea08c6.html

4.4.5 SAP BI with Big Data platforms

The most difficult security and authorization integration is currently the one between the Big Data platform and the SAP BI systems, either SAP HANA native or SAP BW/4HANA. As we have already discussed, the best combination of SAP-based BI and the Big Data platform is via SAP HANA native methods. We will focus on the combination of these two only.

The first point we would like to raise focuses on the necessity of integration. There are three main use cases for accessing the Big Data environment:

1. standard use for specific scenarios or reports for certain departments
2. exploration of data by a data scientist
3. possible definition of new reports or the enhancement of existing reports, by a power user

In the first use case, access and authorizations should be handled through the frontend. Most software products offer the possibility to access the backend through one standard technical user. This removes the need to grant direct access to individual users (e.g. the Big Data platform) and may be sufficient for certain use cases or reports on the platform.

In the second scenario, access to the Big Data platform is required; but the question remains, do any restrictions on the data itself need to be applied? There may be some compliance-related rules, but data scientists mostly need free access to all the data in order to find new relations and connections in it. In order to ensure they have all the data to hand, the data can be copied from the data warehouse to the Big Data platform. This needs to happen anyway when platform is used as an archive, or in a hot-warm-cold storage scenario. This would remove the necessity to give data scientists access to the data warehouse.

Finally, in the third use case, restrictions at data level may need to be applied both on the data warehouse side and on the Big Data side. There is no easy way to ensure that these restrictions are synchronized between the platforms. We see several possibilities for better integration:

- Use LDAP or Active Directory to synchronize users.
- Both Apache Ranger and SAP HANA offer SQL-based privileges and authorizations. An option could be to use the same table within SAP HANA and Hadoop and synchronize this table on a nightly basis, or store it only once and use it across the environments. This table would then contain user names, their assigned roles, what these roles entail, and which tables/columns/files and field values the restriction applies to.

Overall, this solution may work for you, but bear in mind that there is also a performance cost when dynamically looking up the user and applicable privileges.

4.4.6 Cloud security

Cloud security fundamentally relies on the same security and authorization principles as previously described; with some dependencies on your individual architectural setup in the cloud. Nevertheless, some additional measures need to be considered when securing applications and data in a cloud environment. For the hybrid cloud scenario, for instance, we described the connection of an organization's intranet to the cloud platform via VPN tunnels (Section 2.8). However, there are further issues to consider when keeping data in the cloud:

- ▶ Data privacy—The cloud provider potentially stores your customers' or suppliers' data.
- ▶ Data security—Even with strict password regulations, most users still use very unsafe passwords, consisting of short words and some number combinations. Stronger password and protection measures need to be in place when connecting and working in cloud environments
- ▶ User integration—This can also be achieved via directory services such as LDAP, in a secured way.

A whole book could be written about this topic and we will not go into further details here. However, you can refer to further literature on this, such as the homepage of the Cloud Security Alliance (CSA): *https://cloudsecurityalliance.org/research/*

4.5 Change process and training

Introducing a new BI solution or migrating your existing one to a state-of-the-art platform also involves a significant change in your organization. Along with new or changed processes, additional skills are needed in order to use, run, and maintain the solution. We have added this section to underline the importance of sound change management. We now focus on the change process, and training, which are required when introducing, or migrating to, an SAP HANA-enabled BI landscape. Structured change management methods help you to design, implement, and establish the components and processes needed to achieve your BI vision.

No matter which project methodology is applied, most BI projects run over several months or years and they usually cover a wide range of functional subjects and technological components. Proper change management is therefore considered a fundamental discipline in order to introduce modifications, innovations, and enhancements into your organization.

Managing change is an essential and integral part of any BI project. In doing so, you should qualify, and work on, the three dimensions of: **people, technology, and processes**. We do not know your specific business processes, your BI technology preferences, or your staff and its skillset, so we can only provide general guidelines to give you ideas and encourage you to look closer at the changes taking place within your organization.

Before we cover the three dimensions, we want to point out that a key success factor for your SAP HANA BI project is **communication**, which applies to all IT projects and is a core discipline of change management. This includes early stakeholder involvement, including business representatives, and the use of proper channels to address the objective, the roadmap, and next steps of your BI proposition. In addition, you need timely feedback regarding your plans and you have to react accordingly. You need to give progress updates and notification of any adjustments to the plan going forward. The readiness of your organization to accept and implement any planned or adjusted changes should also be continuously cross-checked.

Communication should be seen as elementary across people, processes, and technology. Today, methodical approaches such as design thinking and storytelling assist with effective communication; for example, slipping into the role of a respective user group. From the very beginning, your change management team needs to determine a clear communication plan.

> **SAP Build—boost your enterprise business apps**
>
>  To minimize user communication and integration issues in your development and change process, we refer you to *http://build.me*. Build provides a platform with a comprehensive set of tools for your user interface developments for ideation, prototyping, and gathering feedback (e.g. apps, dashboards). The software supports you in identifying your end users' needs, drafting user stories, creating clickable markups based on your findings from interviews and workshops, turning and refining the clickable markups into prototypes by adding predefined elements from the gallery (e.g. charts), importing data, and gathering direct feedback. This enables a close exchange between the involved parties.

Let's now have a closer look at the three dimensions of change. First, let's look at **people**—they are your staff, and their knowledge is key for the success of your business. They are the ones who conduct the necessary steps that make change happen. Furthermore, they need to understand, accept, and support the new way forward. We again emphasize the importance of communication, and getting involvement and commitment from early on. Your staff also needs to learn what is required of them to support and contribute to the change (i.e. self-reflection). This refers to their own skillset and their willingness to adapt their mindset to the change plan. Only by doing so can they collaborate and integrate with the team and work towards the desired goal (e.g. the new SAP HANA BI landscape). This also means that they accept and effectively use the new (BI) solution in its entirety (i.e. not only from a technological perspective, but also with regard to organizational modifications such as processes or responsibilities). It is essential to identify the knowledge gap and perform the necessary training for each user and stakeholder. At this point, we want to sidetrack a little bit to outline the aspect of **training** as an important element of change management.

The first step with training is to identify and capture the training requirements. Remember that your BI solution most probably will not go live with a big-bang launch; technological components and functionalities will be provided step-by-step. Therefore, the training can be structured alongside your implementation roadmap. This also helps to tailor and group the training content into modules. In addition, when identifying the training requirements you should also think about the necessary resource skills and level mix, if this was not done upfront. Having a clear picture of the qualification profiles needed also helps you to build the training modules. With this information, you can decide who should have what training, based on the skills and levels required in order to gain the necessary knowledge. Alternatively, you can identify which skills you need to obtain externally. Determining the training and resourcing plan is a very helpful part of the entire change process.

When conducting training in previous projects, it was useful to follow a train-the-trainer concept, in order to introduce knowledge into an organization and spread it further. With the train-the-trainer approach, only selected key users receive training; in turn, they act as trainers and further conduct training sessions for end users. The training content should cover both the technology and the supported processes. As a result, the training content is understood much more easily and is more tangible for the participants. It is also beneficial to combine various learning methods to give the training sessions a hands-on, practical base according to the specifics of each unit (e.g. classroom training, e-learning, movies, and hands-on exercises).

In an SAP HANA BI scenario, training is needed for various target groups and for various types of users and skill sets. This should be the first criteria used to define your training modules. End users need training in how to use the solution (e.g. via SAP Business Object tools) whereas developers or operations staff are responsible for building, enhancing, and running the solution (e.g. via SAP HANA Studio, Query Designer, Process Monitors).

In today's modern and mixed reporting and analytics world, there is a wide range of end-user requirements on how to work with data (from executing pre-defined standard reports to developing and executing your own algorithms and routines on the data). The training approach and content have to differ in order to address the needs of each group. We also recommend that the training is not split up into overly-detailed sessions, and that for each individual training demand there is a separate module. One example of sessions at a too-detailed level would be conducting separate training for each data domain and neglecting technically similar setups. It is beneficial to have a high-level training and a few specific modules for the more detailed training.

In addition to grouping by user types, the technological component is also an important aspect when splitting your training requirement into modules. Let's start with the underlying platforms such as SAP HANA and Hadoop for a first grouping. From a technological perspective, they differ significantly. However, both platforms serve data-processing purposes, so at a logical level we see similar ways to structure your training, such as grouping for data ingestion, data processing, data storing, and data provisioning tasks. However, this logical splitting might help you to structure your overall training program. For data ingestion on SAP HANA, you could consider tools such as SLT, SDI, or SAP Data Services, whereas on Hadoop, Kafka, Sqoop, or SAP Data Services might form your training sessions. Remember to think about the respective users of these platforms; for example, data scientists might feel more at home in the plain Big Data world than in the structured, more restricted world of SAP HANA.

> **Standard versus individual custom training**
>
>  Creating training content and associated practical exercises for trainees requires a significant amount of effort. Our recommendation is to start with the standard training which is provided by the tool/software vendors as the first step into the new world. Building small training modules for your specific training scenario is then the logical next move. In doing so, your individual, custom training is reduced to a manageable level.

Before we move on the next important element of change management, we would like to underline the necessity of winning your team's support for the change. Our experience shows that many users feel comfortable with good old SAP BW. They have somehow managed to organize their daily tasks using workarounds to overcome the obstacles of SAP BW-based reporting (e.g. by creating shadow reports in Excel). You need their buy-in, so demonstrate to them the possibilities of the new solution and emphasize how it will minimize or solve existing problems. Furthermore, convince them that SAP BW and the underlying architectural and data modeling approaches have moved towards a lightweight, flexible data warehouse with a modern, user-friendly interface. Ideally, you should demonstrate this with a working prototype so that end users can experience the new features on their own.

Coming back to our three dimensions of change management, we'll next look at **technology** The main thing to remember is that that technology is there to enable your staff to perform their daily work to the best possible level, and to support and contribute to your business processes in the best possible way. Nevertheless, your people must understand, accept, and adopt the new technology, otherwise, the effort and investment to establish a new technological BI platform is wasted and the capabilities of the new solution are only partially leveraged. In the worst case, this could mean that a large portion of your endeavors are not utilized for your daily business. As mentioned earlier, this can easily be achieved by involving your stakeholders in the project as early as possible, and explaining the benefits of the upcoming technological change right from the beginning; you need to get them on side.

In addition to the new technological solution, a suitable collaboration platform also needs to be introduced, giving all involved parties a centralized environment to provide the latest updates and new functional content, and to provide information about upcoming events or appointments.

Last, but not least, change is about improving business **processes**. In BI projects, do not underestimate the impact on your transactional and analytical processes. Reporting and analytical processes should run more efficiently and provide additional options in addition to those which were available before. This must be understood and accepted by your team. Today, transactional and analytical systems work more closely together. Data-generating systems can directly benefit from insights derived from analytical environments. Specific business areas can now be managed in a more targeted way. A good example is SAP Fiori tiles, which can be personalized according to the tasks given to a selected user. The crucial point here is that employees no longer need to execute and analyze numerous standard reports, but rather have their relevant KPIs available at a glance. They therefore only need to look into those areas in which the KPI values are out of range.

The process of change management also serves the need to control and monitor the ongoing change itself. Therefore, suitable tools and the above-mentioned collaboration platforms can be supportive here.

> **SAP Solution Manager**
>
>  SAP Solution Manager can be a key support for your ongoing move towards a new SAP HANA BI platform, especially at a technological level. In almost all SAP-related transformation and change programs, our clients have used additional collaboration tools such as Sharepoint, Jira, and Confluence to set up, execute, monitor, and control the progress of their change program.

In summary, do not underestimate the importance of solid change management right at the beginning of your SAP HANA BI project. This is especially valid for small or medium-sized projects where companies are more likely to skip the sometimes unpleasant activities of change management. Expectation management is also essential; with a new BI solution, not everything is automatically simpler and easier. Users have to accept new ways of working, and they need a willingness to learn and use the new technology. Our experience shows that this is often not the case. You need to implement a rigorous change management process, in order to increase the effectiveness and efficiency of your team's work towards your BI goals; in turn, this enables you to further enhance the performance of your actual business.

4.6 Summary

Introducing a new SAP HANA-based BI solution, or migrating an existing one, requires your full attention; and not only at a technical level. We therefore focused this chapter on often-undervalued topics which could significantly affect your organization during your BI landscape transformation. We discussed several topics to help you avoid loss of efficiency in your daily business processes, and to ensure that the new BI solution is leveraged to its full extent:

- ▶ Landscape enablement—we emphasized the importance of a well-thought-out roadmap for your BI vision.

- Data Governance—we presented important areas such as data lineage, metadata management, data quality, data security, and business processes, and we highlighted the challenges in a hybrid BI environment.
- Development guidelines—we talked about parallel development, debugging, and end-to-end testing in combined SAP and Big Data environments. Furthermore, we touched on considerations regarding the transfer of developments in an SAP BI/Big Data eco system.
- Security and authorizations—we discussed concepts and practices in various scenarios such as SAP HANA only, hybrid scenarios with various SAP components, and combined solutions with Big Data or Cloud elements.
- Change process and training—we explained the three dimensions of change management (people, technology, and processes), and discussed key considerations and recommendations for training.

5 Summary and outlook

In this final chapter, we recap the key findings in this book and take a future-oriented look at topics and trends for further research. We also encourage you to get in touch with us to discuss current and future SAP HANA architecture issues. Best practices and solid architectural solutions are achieved with constant communication with your peers to open your mind to incorporate different perspectives into your vision of a modern SAP HANA BI architecture.

5.1 Summary

Leveraging our hands-on project experience and findings from comprehensive research and test scenarios, we provided an overview of architectural components regarding SAP HANA BI landscapes and made recommendations on how to model SAP HANA BI architectures. We considered and highlighted technological and functional requirements of the intended solution, the current market development regarding technologies and analytics trends, as well as SAP's strategy. We showed which architectural elements to use for which purpose, and which scenarios to follow for specific requirements and environments. We detailed and evaluated typical use case scenarios. Finally, we pointed out the impact to your organization and the steps necessary to deal with the entire change management process

In the introduction, we set the scene, and outlined the objective of this book. In Chapter 2, we started to examine the building blocks of SAP HANA-based BI architectures. The objective of this chapter was to build a basic understanding for subsequent architectural discussions.

After a brief view of the SAP HANA engines, we introduced Extended Application Services (XSA) and the SAP HANA deployment infrastructure (HDI). We finished the first part of the chapter with the latest updates on modeling with SAP HANA views, and utilizing new functionalities and libraries.

In the next section on embedded analytics, we highlighted the possibilities with SAP S/4HANA, which also impact analytics scenarios. The functionality and content of SAP S/4HANA Embedded Analytics were also discussed under the spotlight of modern SAP HANA BI architectures. We then detailed the reform of SAP BW. We explained in detail the architectural and data model aspects of SAP BW/4HANA and their strong integration with SAP S/4HANA. Within this topic, we also covered infrastructure-related considerations such as on-premise versus cloud, and gave tips for migration scenarios.

A popular hot topic is development in the area of Big Data technology. After a general definition, we introduced key components of a Big Data ecosystem and put them into an architectural framework. We also mentioned the Lambda architecture approach. One key point from this section was the combination of Big Data with SAP HANA technology. After evaluating typical use case scenarios, we presented common technological approaches to bring these two worlds together.

Closely linked to SAP HANA and Big Data, are analytics approaches and methods. We took a closer look at predictive analytics languages and components such as R, SAP Predictive Analytics (PA), and the SAS Workbench for SAP HANA.

The cloud is currently an intensely debated topic, so we dedicated a separate section to this. We differentiated the cloud offerings (IaaS, PaaS, SaaS) and linked them to the associated SAP solutions (e.g. SAP Cloud Platform, SAP Analytics Cloud). In concluding this section, we stated the typical drivers and benefits of cloud offerings.

As part of any architectural discussion, we also presented options for building your frontend. In addition to the well-known SAP Business Objects Suite, modern approaches leveraging SAP Fiori or SAP UI5 technology were an integral part of this section. Many SAP-based BI systems also use non-SAP front-end products, and we discussed and assessed front-end tools such as Tableau, QlikView, and Microsoft Power BI.

We closed Chapter 2 with a description of typical data provisioning tools for batch and streaming functionality. We introduced products such as SAP Data Services, Smart Data Integration, and SAP Data Streaming, as well as non-SAP products such as Sqoop and Kafka. At that point, we also pointed out the importance of checking and controlling data quality (e.g. by using SAP Information Steward).

In Chapter 3, we provided a reference architecture, which encompasses three foundational layers: data generation, data digestion and storage, and data consumption. This high-level grouping enables you to structure and break down your SAP HANA BI initiative.

The chapter started by looking at SAP BW/4HANA. One of the main topics was the new data transfer mechanisms and which option was best for which situation. There have also been some fundamental changes in the data modeling object types, so we dedicated a separate section to data modeling in SAP BW/4HANA because it can influence your overall architectural design. We also pointed out the benefits of SAP BW and how to migrate to the latest SAP BW version.

SAP HANA native components are closely associated with SAP BW/4HANA. Therefore, we added a depiction of a standard SAP HANA native data flow. We further outlined how the XSA engine helps you to administer your SAP HANA native solution (e.g. for error-handling, monitoring, job scheduling). We closed this section with by comparing SAP HANA native to SAP BW/4HANA.

Next, we focused on the first combined scenario and described which technological components can be utilized in order to connect SAP HANA and Big Data. As well as the reference architecture, we defined three use cases (data federation, data aging, data lake). After presenting the objective and technological approach of each use case, we provided a comprehensive comparison of the key differentiators. We identified challenges such as technical integration, authorization, data loading, and the synchronization of developments. We finished this section by looking at the drivers and benefits of a combined scenario.

Predictive analytics is increasingly becoming a key element of a re-designed, or newly-designed, SAP HANA BI landscape, and we detailed the specifics of the combined scenario. After outlining the architectural setup, we used the layers of the reference architecture to explain components and data modeling aspects that you need to keep in mind when constructing your analytics solution. We summarized general aspects (e.g. data quality, variable creation, external and unstructured sources) and administrative aspects (e.g. model management, scheduling and monitoring), which we consider to be important. We finished this section by outlining the reasons for taking a step towards predictive analytics.

The next part of this chapter looked at questions relating to SAP HANA in the cloud. User security, company intranet connectivity, patching, and upgrade mechanisms in the cloud were fundamental discussion points before we dived deeper into data acquisition, remote synchronization and examples of applications in the cloud.

One of the most important parts of this book was the section about mixed scenarios. We presented three architectural scenarios which we recently explored in our practical work, and which we see a great demand for in the future. These were: Hybrid SAP BW and SAP HANA native scenario, SAP HANA with Big Data and analytics, and the IoT end-to-end scenario. For each scenario, we used the reference architecture to explain the technical solution, drivers, challenges and pitfalls, and we finished with a critical appraisal.

Based on the previous learnings, we outlined the general options on how to migrate from an existing BI solution to a new one. In this section, Greenfield, Brownfield, and 1:1 migration options were discussed, assessed and compared.

At the end of the chapter we included best practice recommendations to give you a structured guideline towards your SAP HANA BI target state. We consolidated our learnings and research results into a decision matrix to help you determine technological component setups and methodological approaches in order to best fulfill your specific requirements.

In Chapter 4, we described general organizational principles and principles with respect to SAP HANA BI architectures. We started with basic aspects to kick off your initiative and prepare your landscape for the upcoming change. Here, we focused on the roadmap, interfaces, and responsibilities, which stakeholders have to agree on.

Next, we looked in detail at Data Governance. Data lineage, data quality, metadata management, and data security are considered crucial for the success of your BI project and were therefore covered in detail.

The section on development environment focused on concepts of parallel development, including in a hybrid or mixed SAP HANA BI architecture. The key words here were modularization, data synthesizing, and close cooperation. Debugging, end-to-end testing, and transport and deployment of objects were also important parts of this section.

Without a proper security and authorization concept, you cannot bring your SAP HANA BI architecture to life. Therefore, key decision points were discussed and recommendations were given, based on our experiences.

At the end of Chapter 4, we discussed change management and training, and took a close look at people, technology and processes. Your team needs to use the new SAP HANA BI solution, so acceptance and training to enable your staff are crucial elements of change management.

Chapter 5 served as a summary of this book and looks into the future of upcoming SAP HANA BI technologies and trends.

5.2 Outlook

The rise of Big Data technologies has opened a large area of previously unknown analytical features and ways of working with massive amounts of data; a new generation of very promising technologies and approaches to handle data is imminent.

5.2.1 SAP Data Hub

SAP Data Hub was released in 2017 (see Section 3.7.2) The features within SAP Data Hub promise an end-to-end management of data landscapes, including Big Data technologies. It deals with on-premise, cloud, and hybrid solutions. Throughout your data environment, the SAP Data Hub provides capabilities for data pipelines, data discovery, and orchestration of data pumps. In parallel, access control and hub management features help you to organize and monitor your overall data landscape.

> **Feature overview—SAP Data Hub**
>
>  Additional information about the features and capabilities of SAP Data Hub are available at:
>
> *https://www.sap.com/products/data-hub/features.html.*

We also recognize that with the increasing maturity of SAP HANA and Big Data technologies, the demand for real-time data processing and event streaming is steadily growing. Understanding and handling the requirements and challenges of this discipline opens up a wide field of research; for example, the join and transformation of streaming data on the fly, the full traceability for audit requirements, or the correct resumption of event streams in case of failure. However, with the continuous growth of the technological stacks for BI solutions, we will continue to look curiously towards streaming data warehouses and the vision to one day run all analytics on virtual models, in real-time.

5.2.2 SAP Leonardo

With SAP Leonardo, SAP has addressed a whole range of new and upcoming technologies. Some of them (e.g. IoT and Big Data) were discussed in detail in this book, and their usage in real-life scenarios was covered in Section 3.7. The ability to use data from sensors, or information from devices interacting with each other in analytic scenarios, is currently being explored by many organizations and is becoming an integral part of research studies. A well-thought-out combination of Big Data and in-memory technologies is the basis for getting the most out of this massive amount of data.

From our perspective, the IoT momentum and the growth of Big Data are now about to mature and their full contribution and potential for analytics will be seen in the next few years. In addition to understanding the underlying technologies, we see major challenges in getting the right information out of the data lake at the right time, and accurately combining it with your internal ERP or CRM data. We therefore see a need for support, not only at technological level, but also with regard to functional, regulatory, and security questions; for example—Which data am I allowed to combine or store? Which is the correct aggregation level for combining the information? How long is a specific value valid?

SAP Leonardo also covers emerging technologies such as Blockchain. Blockchain uses cryptography to link and secure data blocks in a continuously growing list. As each block has a hash-based pointer to its predecessor (as well as its actual data and timestamp information), the rising chain is resistant to any change or manipulation. In the finance area in particular, Blockchain is currently being evaluated with high expectations because it is a trusted, open and distributed ledger. Managed by peers in a joint network, the chain is collectively enhanced by new validated records (blocks). With blockchain, the lack of trust between intermediary parties is addressed. We believe that cases for Blockchain are not limited to the finance sector. We see it as an approach to secure and store transactional information in any business, or even private, area.

> **Reading material: Blockchain**
>
>
> An appropriate definition of Blockchain as an "open, distributed ledger that can record transactions between two parties efficiently and in a verifiable and permanent way" is available in the Harvard Business Review article "The Truth about Blockchain". This article gives a critical appraisal of this technology and can be found at:
> https://hbr.org/2017/01/the-truth-about-blockchain.
>
> We also recommend reading the following Gartner contribution "A Snapshot of an Emerging Blockchain Services Market" at:
>
> https://www.gartner.com/smarterwithgartner/a-snapshot-of-an-emerging-blockchain-services-market/.

In addition, SAP has recognized the potential of Blockchains. Looking at ERP systems, for example, in which millions of transactions are posted every day, why not think about blockchain mechanisms to ease and secure transactions between your business counterparts and your organization (e.g. in a supply chain scenario)? SAP is currently running pilots providing Blockchain-as-a-Service (BaaS) via the SAP Cloud Platform.

> **SAP Blockchain-as-a-Service (BaaS)**
>
>  SAP's Blockchain offering and the latest updates are available at:
>
> https://www.sap.com/products/leonardo/blockchain.html#

Another interesting aspect of SAP Leonardo is Data Intelligence. With Data Intelligence, SAP addresses the monetization of your internal data. The insights gained from analysis and analytics on your data should enable you to expand services and the areas in which you do business. The term Data Intelligence is open to interpretation. We want to point out that several data-driven approaches such as advanced analytics, event processing, and business performance assessments can play an integral part in Data Intelligence.

> **Recommended reading: analytics goes mainstream**
>
>  We recommend reading the following Gartner article about the potential growth of analytics, on its way to becoming a mainstream discipline:
>
> https://www.gartner.com/smarterwithgartner/2017-the-year-that-data-and-analytics-go-mainstream/

Following SAP's interpretation of Data Intelligence, the monetization of insights gathered from analytics applications has come to the fore. SAP foresees solutions to enable, for example, a Data-as-a-Service (DaaS) revenue stream, data insights services or data-driven apps for your business partners. The actual benefit and potential that these services and apps will bring has yet to be proven. Leveraging your data to increase revenue, by either directly or indirectly expanding your business, is a long-cherished dream, which has already come true to some extent.

A further influencer of the future characteristic of SAP analytics solutions that must not be ignored is the push towards cloud-based services and solutions. Also SAP adapted this trend and released new features firstly (and partly also exclusively) on its cloud products. Some software like the SAP Analytics Cloud is even only available as a Cloud solution.

> **SAP Data Intelligence**
>
>  More details about SAP's view and vision on Data Intelligence can be found at:
>
> *https://www.sap.com/products/leonardo/data-intelligence-monetization.html.*

Thinking about Artificial Intelligence (AI) as a next level of analytics, the future role and growth potential for SAP HANA is an amazing field of research. Artificial intelligence has existed for several decades (back in the 1950's, there was an idea of thinking machines). Later in the 1980's, the first steps were taken, in what we now know as "machine learning", to enhance computers with technology, allowing them to learn and prove intelligence in their results. Typical use cases are prediction scenarios in a pre-defined subject. The basis for this is often domain models, which have been trained upfront or were trained by the machines. Neuronal networks and deep learning algorithms made further research into machine learning possible. Finally, cognitive computing came into play, looking towards solutions with a natural interaction of machines and humans (motivated by, and combined with, a strong learning curve on the machine side). SAP is also looking into tangible assets using research results from these disciplines.

5.2.3 Big Data

We also see an unrestricted growth and further application of Big Data technologies. On one hand, this involves the utilization of existing tools; for example, for more streaming scenarios (there is already some talk about streaming data warehouses). Spark, Spark Streaming and Kafka are currently examples of this and most likely new Apache projects will also be published. On the other hand, the technology stack itself is being enhanced and new feature updates are repeatedly published (e.g. Apache Hadoop 3.0.0). The updated features and effects on existing projects and tools are currently being widely discussed.

> **Updates on Hadoop 3.0**
>
>  The latest release notes and feature information about Hadoop 3.0 are available at:
>
> *https://cwiki.apache.org/confluence/display/HADOOP/Hadoop+3.0.0+release*
>
> and *https://hadoop.apache.org/docs/r3.1.1/*.

Looking at the current momentum and speed at which analytics is evolving and growing, we foresee a thrilling and fascinating future for BI with SAP HANA. How to leverage and build your future SAP HANA BI landscape will remain a major question.

You have finished the book.

Sign up for our newsletter!

Want to learn more about new e-books? Get exclusive free downloads and SAP tips. Sign up for our newsletter!

Please visit us at *newsletter.espresso-tutorials.com* to find out more.

A About the Authors

Dominique Alfermann has been working in various lead and architectural roles in SAP Analytics projects for the last 6 years. In these roles, he has led development and delivery teams, and has frequently consulted clients on major architectural decisions in the SAP analytics area. Most recently, he has started consulting on cutting-edge hybrid Big Data and SAP analytics projects in architectural and lead roles.

Dr. Stefan Hartmann has been successfully leading and executing (SAP) Analytics transformation programs for more than 15 years. He is a highly qualified architect, and also works as a program manager. In recent years, he has designed and built innovative, leading-edge analytical applications utilizing both core SAP components and trendsetting technologies such as Big Data, Internet of Things (IoT) and Blockchain. Dr. Hartmann is recognized for his expert knowledge in designing modern, future-ready analytics solutions which bring the best of various technological worlds together.

B Index

1
1:1 Migration 170, 173

A
ABAP Managed Database Procedures (AMDP) 41, 108
Active Directory 125, 142, 207
Advanced Data Store Object (ADSO) 39, 106
Analysis for Microsoft Office 62
Analytic Manager 112
Analytics 53, 155, 158
Apache Hadoop 70
Apache Kafka 52
Apache Ranger 193, 204, 207
Architected Data Marts 91
Authorizations 125, 150, 192, 200

B
BI Architecture 16
Big Data 69, 88, 114, 155, 165, 206, 225
Big Data platform Predictive Models 133
Blockchain 223
Bring Your Own Language (BYOL) 24
Brownfield Migration 170, 174
Business Intelligence (BI) 15
Business Planning and Consolidation (BPC) 45, 87, 88

C
CDS Views 23, 44, 90, 103
Change Management 209
Cloud Platform 35, 77, 141
Cloud Security 208
Cognitive Computing 225
Composite Provider 41, 107
Core Data Services (CDS) 30
Corporate Memory 155

D
Data Aging 116
Data Federation 115
Data Flow Modeler 41, 109
Data Governance 187
Data Intelligence 224
Data Lake 70, 117, 155
Data Lineage 188
Data Loads 125
Data Quality 188
Data Security 190, 192, 200
Data Synthesizing 196
Data Warehouse 16
Debugging 197
Design Studio 62
DevOps 185
Dynamic Tiering 41

E
End-to-End Testing 198
Extraction, Load and Transformation (ELT) 46

Extraction, Transformation and Load (ETL) 16, 46

F
Front-end Tools 150, 158

G
Greenfield Migration 170

H
HDFS 71
Hybrid Cloud Architecture 80, 145, 200

I
Infrastructure-as-a-Service (IAAS) 81
Integrated Planning (IP) 45
Internet of Things (IoT) 161
IoT Connector 162

L
Lightweight Directory Access Protocol (LDAP) 125, 142, 204, 207
LSA++ Architecture 40, 87, 106
Lumira 62

M
Machine Learning 225
MapReduce 70
MATLAB 60
Metadata Management 126, 189
Microsoft Power BI 66
Migration 43
Modularization 194

N
Native Datastore Object (NDSO) 97
Nearline Storage (NLS) 43, 112

O
On-premise 35, 78
Open ODS View 41, 106
Operational Data Provisioning (ODP) 43, 44, 102, 152
Operational Delta Queue (ODQ) 44

P
Parallel Development 193
Planning Application Kit (PAK) 45
Platform-as-a-Service (PaaS) 81, 143
Predictive Analytics
   Hybrid solution 133
Private Cloud 79
Public Cloud 79

Q
Qlik Sense 65
QlikView 65

R
R 54
Referential Integrity 96
Remote Data Sync 147

S
SAP Analytics Cloud 82
SAP Business ByDesign 103
SAP BusinessObjects 61
SAP BW embedded 111

Index

SAP BW/4HANA 38, 87, 102, 148, 155, 204, 206
SAP BW/4HANA Migration 113
SAP Cloud Big Data Services 159
SAP Cloud Connector 145, 165
SAP Cloud Platform (SCP) 79, 142, 162
SAP Cloud Platform IoT Services 162
SAP Data Hub 159, 221
SAP Data Lifecycle Manager (DLM) 123
SAP Data Services 44, 47, 76, 158
SAP Enterprise Information Management (EIM) 44, 89, 96
SAP Event Stream Processor 164
SAP Fiori 34, 64, 206, 213
SAP HANA Analysis Processes 41
SAP HANA Analytical Privileges 206
SAP HANA Authorization Concepts 205
SAP HANA BI Reference Architecture 85
SAP HANA Data Warehousing Foundation 92, 94, 97, 101
SAP HANA Deployment Infrastructure (HDI) 27
SAP HANA Engines 22
SAP HANA Enterprise Cloud (HEC) 42
SAP HANA Extension Nodes 42
SAP HANA Flow Graph 90
SAP HANA Libraries 31
SAP HANA Native 87, 88, 148, 155, 206
SAP HANA Real-Time Connection 89
SAP HANA Source System 44, 104
SAP HANA Spark Controller 75
SAP HANA Spatial Engine 31
SAP HANA Studio 42
SAP HANA Text Analysis 32
SAP HANA Views 29
SAP Identity Manager 203
SAP Information Steward 49
SAP Landscape Transformation Replication (SLT) 44, 103
SAP Leonardo 168, 222
SAP Master Data Governance 189
SAP Predictive Analytics 56, 98
SAP S/4HANA 33, 87, 204
SAP S/4HANA Embedded Analytics 37, 87, 111, 150
SAP S/4HANA Finance 34
SAP Solution Manager 214
SAP Vora 76, 156
SAPUI5 63
SAS Predictive Modeling Workbench 59
SAS Predictive Modeling Workbench for SAP HANA 134
Service Level Agreement (SLA) 185
Sizing 185
Smart Data Access (SDA) 75, 104, 156

231

Smart Data Integration (SDI) 25, 44, 49, 90, 93, 104
Smart Data Quality (SDQ) 49
Smart Data Streaming (SDS) 52, 98, 164
Software-as-a-Service (SaaS) 82, 143
Spark 72
SPSS Modeler 60
SQL Engine 23
Sqoop 50, 72, 76
Streaming 51
Synchronization of Developments 125

T
Tableau 64

V
Virtual Data Mart 92

W
Web Development Workbench (Web IDE) 43, 92
WebIntelligence (WebI) 61
wide format 128

X
XS Engine 22
XSA Engine 24, 63, 92

C Disclaimer

This publication contains references to the products of SAP SE.

SAP, R/3, SAP NetWeaver, Duet, PartnerEdge, ByDesign, SAP BusinessObjects Explorer, StreamWork, and other SAP products and services mentioned herein as well as their respective logos are trademarks or registered trademarks of SAP SE in Germany and other countries.

Business Objects and the Business Objects logo, BusinessObjects, Crystal Reports, Crystal Decisions, Web Intelligence, Xcelsius, and other Business Objects products and services mentioned herein as well as their respective logos are trademarks or registered trademarks of Business Objects Software Ltd. Business Objects is an SAP company.

Sybase and Adaptive Server, iAnywhere, Sybase 365, SQL Anywhere, and other Sybase products and services mentioned herein as well as their respective logos are trademarks or registered trademarks of Sybase, Inc. Sybase is an SAP company.

SAP SE is neither the author nor the publisher of this publication and is not responsible for its content. SAP Group shall not be liable for errors or omissions with respect to the materials. The only warranties for SAP Group products and services are those that are set forth in the express warranty statements accompanying such products and services, if any. Nothing herein should be construed as constituting an additional warranty.

More Espresso Tutorials Books

Rob Frye, Joe Darlak, Dr. Bjarne Berg:

The SAP® BW to HANA Migration Handbook

- ▶ Proven Techniques for Planning and Executing a Successful Migration
- ▶ SAP BW on SAP HANA Sizing and Optimization
- ▶ Building a Solid Migration Business Case
- ▶ Step-by-Step Runbook for the Migration Process

http://5109.espresso-tutorials.com

Dominique Alfermann, Stefan Hartmann, Benedikt Engel:

SAP® HANA Advanced Modeling

- ▶ Data modeling guidelines and common test approaches
- ▶ Modular solutions to complex requirements
- ▶ Information view performance optimization
- ▶ Best practices and recommendations

http://5110.espresso-tutorials.com

Christian Savelli:

SAP® BW on SAP HANA

- ▶ Tips for upgrading, maintaining, and running BW on HANA
- ▶ Data loading methods and real-time data acquisition
- ▶ New reporting paradigm for BW on HANA
- ▶ HANA data architecture

http://5128.espresso-tutorials.com

Deepa Rawat:

Practical Guide to Advanced DSOs in SAP®

- ▶ Fundamentals of Advanced Data Store Objects
- ▶ Modeling with SAP HANA Studio
- ▶ How to create an SAP HANA-optimized InfoProvider
- ▶ Examples and screenshots based on real-world scenarios

http://5213.espresso-tutorials.com

Frank Riesner, Klaus-Peter Sauer:

SAP® BW/4HANA and BW on HANA

- ▶ Migration, sizing, operation, data management with SAP BW/4HANA and SAP BW 7.5 on HANA
- ▶ The new central source Systems SAP HANA and ODP
- ▶ New modeling options, mixed scenarios, LSA++, and differences compared to SAP BW 7.5
- ▶ The role of BW in operational SAP reporting

http://5215.espresso-tutorials.com

Bert Vanstechelman:

The SAP® HANA Implementation Guide

- ▶ SAP HANA sizing, capacity planning guidelines, and data tiering
- ▶ Deployment options and data provisioning scenarios
- ▶ Backup and recovery options and procedures
- ▶ Software and hardware virtualization in SAP HANA

http://5289.espresso-tutorials.com

www.ingramcontent.com/pod-product-compliance
Lightning Source LLC
Chambersburg PA
CBHW052037300426
44117CB00012B/1864